How to Motivate Your Team to Perform

by
Rich Burghgraef

© Global Professional Publishing 2011

Apart from any fair dealing for the purpose of research or private study, or criticism or review, as permitted under the Copyright, Designs and Patents Act 1988, this publication may only be reproduced, stored or transmitted, in any form or by any means, with the prior permission in writing of the publisher, or in the case of reprographic reproduction in accordance with the terms and licences issued by the Copyright Licensing Agency. Enquiries concerning reproduction outside those terms should be addressed to the publisher. The address is below:

Global Professional Publishing
Random Acres
Slip Mill Lane
Hawkhurst
Cranbrook
Kent TN18 5AD
Email: publishing@gppbooks.com

Global Professional Publishing believes that the sources of information upon which the book is based are reliable, and has made every effort to ensure the complete accuracy of the text. However, neither Global Professional Publishing, the authors nor any contributors can accept any legal responsibility whatsoever for consequences that may arise from errors or omissions or any opinion or advice given.

ISBN 978 1 906403 67 6

Printed by Berforts in the United Kingdom

Table of Contents

Introduction 1

Chapter 1:
Hit the Ground Running 3

Chapter 2:
Create a Supportive Environment 23

Chapter 3:
Empower Your Staff 41

Chapter 4:
Provide Direction and Discipline 63

Chapter 5:
Overcome Obstacles 77

Appendix I:
The Resources 95

Introduction

Tens of thousands of pages are written each year about management–the good, the bad and the ugly. The latest theories are presented, analyzed and recommended. Managers virtually swoon from information overload. What is the best way to lead your team? How do you get employees to perform their best, day in and day out? What does senior management expect from your team and from you as a manager? Will one mistake ruin your chances for advancement?

The simple fact is that there is not any one right way to manage; but there are some very good, basic concepts that, if incorporated into individualized management strategies, tend to outlast all of the other nonsense that is out there. Top managers motivate their employees from day one. They understand that leading workers to deliver superior performance day in, day out requires a commitment to clear communication, consistent support and sound judgment. Common sense? Perhaps. More likely it is learned behavior that rewards workers, instills confidence in your judgment and enhances the quality and importance of the work to be done.

In this Business Best book, you will learn how to build a team of loyal, driven employees who trust you and respect your leadership. Each chapter is designed to help sharpen your management savvy by giving you easy-to-apply tools. Examples include pointers on setting goals, enforcing rules and spurring innovation.

A common theme throughout this book is the importance of planning. Because each day brings new challenges for managers, it is wise to anticipate problems and craft strategies to address them. If you know how to overcome obstacles before they arise, you can plow ahead confidently when it matters most.

What is more, by listening closely and empathizing with your staff, you will promote good will and prevent misunderstandings. By modeling the kind of behavior you desire of your employees, you will reinforce your integrity and fairness. Everyone will want to follow your lead.

Because you are attentive and sensitive, does that mean that everything will always go smoothly? Of course not; there will be times when you hire the wrong person, there is a bad mix in the team or you yourself fail to follow your own or company guidelines. The simple fact is that things happen which you cannot control; the goal of this book is to focus your attention on the dozens of small, everyday matters that you can control. You thereby gain a statistical edge in the business of management—you reduce the chances of serious error because you have both planned for events and have anticipated what you might do if they actually occur.

Be forceful, be strong and assertive, but also be thoughtful and analytical. Spend your time on what can be controlled and use your personal and company resources wisely and prudently.

Hit the Ground Running

NEWCOMERS NEED EXTRA HELP STARTING OUT

There is a terrible time gap between when an individual is hired and when she is actually productive and a functioning member of the team or department. This is not an easy time for anyone, especially the newly hired employee. Assuming you have hired the best you can afford (or budgeted for), the burden is on you (or selected team members) to make sure that this hiring process works.

Once you have selected the best candidate to fill a job opening, you should lay the groundwork right away for the newcomer to succeed. Do not leave anything to chance.

Smart managers know that putting new hires through an orientation program is not enough. That is why a new kind of initiation program, called the rapid assimilation process, has gained popularity. The process involves three steps:

1. Peers and staff who will work with the new hire meet to share their concerns and ideas about the challenges the newcomer will face. The facilitator (usually an HR rep or outside consultant) takes notes on issues raised by the group. Their comments are kept anonymous.

2. The new hire meets privately with the facilitator to review the group's input and confirm her understanding of their points.

3. The new hire meets with the group and addresses their concerns. "This process increases productivity and gives new hires a chance to lay out their strategic plans and go over their management style," says Regan Traub, president of The Human Resource Consortium, a consulting firm in New Haven, Conn. "It makes it easier for everyone to start off on the same page."

Even with an effective rapid assimilation process in place, the person you have hired—who is all too aware of how difficult it has been to find a job—might be tense, nervous and cautious. You are backlogged with work and want results immediately. Your staff, who may be overburdened and perhaps anxious about their own jobs, may either expect too much of the new person or even attempt to thwart his success.

POINTING THE WAY

To help the newcomer produce results smoothly and quickly, you need to point the way. Some key steps to take:

- Do the welcoming aboard personally. This will signal to your staff your support for the newcomer. Whether by e-mail or in a staff meeting, briefly explain the new hire's background and qualifications and why she was brought on board. (This will help allay any fears or rumors that someone may be replaced.) Make it clear that you expect the staff to help the newcomer get up to speed and that you highly value everyone's assistance.

- Lengthen the orientation. Rather than devote the newcomer's first day to an intensive orientation, ration out information over the first week or two. If you heap too much information on the employee on Day 1, chances are most of it would not stick. It is better to complete the high-priority tasks upfront, such as an explanation of benefits and enrollment in group insurance, and leave everything else to later.

- Supply more than the standard office essentials. Make sure the newcomer has an internal phone list, an organizational chart and samples of your organization's products or services as well as any introductory literature or files that are relevant to the job and to the organization's mission. Also, supply and explain work schedules, report forms, work analyses and other essentials.

Business Best Tip:
Avoid orientation programs in which an HR rep spends hours leading newcomers page by page through the employee handbook. Instead, give them a copy of the handbook to read within, say, one week and ask them to sign an acknowledgment that they have done so.

- Include the new person in meetings, both formal and informal. This enables the newcomer to see people in action and get to know them. Meetings also give her the opportunity to participate, which you should encourage. This shows the new hire, as well as the rest of your staff, that you view her as a full-fledged member of your team from the start.

- Look into training possibilities. If your organization has a training program, find out how it could benefit the new employee. Otherwise, design your own program tailored to the particular demands of the job. You might, for example, give initial work assignments with an eye toward providing the broadest base of experience. Or you might recommend reading specific books or periodicals. Also consider providing a mentor, a staff member who can guide and encourage the new person.

- Maintain regular contact. The newcomer should feel that your door is always open. You might have a regularly scheduled time together, a few minutes of the day or a half hour or so each week. Or offer him a standing invitation to bring questions or concerns to you whenever they arise.

Business Best Observation
If, like so many managers, you have been working without a full staff, you know how important it is to make sure every new hire succeeds. The greater the effort you make now, the sooner you will begin to see a payoff.

ON-BOARDING: GOING BEYOND THE BASICS IN WELCOMING EMPLOYEES

Michael O'Malley, author of the book, *Creating Commitment*, says there are two goals for new employee on-boarding: to get people as socially and technically proficient as possible so they can be useful at work and to help them feel like part of the team. On-boarding is different from the basic orientation that is described above. First, on-boarding helps familiarize employees with their roles, the organization, its employees and policies. Second, on-boarding enables socialization to the values, norms and beliefs held by the organization.

On-boarding (or employee orientation program) can be effective if managers:

- Create a formal process, but also ensure that it is enjoyable.
- Recognize that on-boarding takes time.
- Use online tools whenever possible, especially with younger, computer-savvy employees.
- Identify and outline clearly the supervisor's role in the process.
- Create a new hire mentor program.
- Measure your progress by quantifying results.

CREATING LOYAL EMPLOYEES

Personal and professional loyalty is a concept that is both powerful and admired. The problem is that it is increasingly hard to find these days. Using professional sports as an example, players used to stay with a team for their entire career, often later joining the ranks of assistant coaches or even the broadcast booth. These days, fans have to open the newspaper to find out who is still on the team from last year!

The business environment was much the same. Years ago, younger employees would stay on a job for experience for several years before venturing on; it was not uncommon for someone to work for a company for 20 or 30 years, even retiring from the company without every having changed employers. The current trend is for people in their 20s and 30s to stay just long enough to get a better job, based on their experience and training. In addition to the lack of loyalty, the expense of a highly mobile workforce can be huge, especially for small- and mid-sized companies.

Loyalty can be an abstraction, very hard to define and even harder to foster. Loyalty is primarily the relationship between the individual team member and the company, or more probably, the team and its manager. Loyalty is a contract and is often the reason people stay with a company, particularly during difficult times. Loyalty is needed if a team is to succeed in its most basic goals.

HOW TO FOSTER LOYALTY TO THE TEAM AND THE COMPANY

Stephen Robbins, the author of *Organizational Behavior*, says that the most important part of fostering team loyalty is the manager herself. It is all about you—how you behave, how you react under stress and how you treat team members. Employees are more often loyal to their bosses and the team than the company itself.

As a manager or a business owner, you will instill loyalty if you can demonstrate that you have what it takes to run the department or keep the company going. You need to demonstrate competence on the everyday business level and you need to show leadership and commitment. Loyalty is, in part, based on whether they respect you as a person and as a manager. (Notice liking you is not necessarily an issue.)

The second biggest component of loyalty is personal integrity and a general sense of fairness. While it is human nature to blame others, a good team leader fosters loyalty by taking the blame when she is wrong. Further, you treat everyone equally as far as you can. Nothing makes people crazier than when one team member gets special treatment—extra time off or easy assignments—and the other members do not.

Simple honesty and business ethics are also a huge part of building and maintaining loyalty. Who wants to work for someone who does not follow the rules or takes personal or financial advantage of loopholes; very few people do. They need to think of their boss as an ethical person. There are times when telling the truth can be very awkward, but it needs to be done. Loyal team members want to hear the truth, even if it is unpleasant.

A major flaw of some managers is that they have not learned the value—the necessity—of protecting their team members and helping them save face. That does not mean that you do not have the right and the obligation to correct or reprimand an employee or to correct business practices. Of course you do and you should. But it is in how you do this—calmly, fairly and in private—that is so important to both helping the employee grow and fostering a loyal team member. Anyone and everyone can take correction, direction or even discipline if it is done objectively and fairly. Resist the urge to charge out and make accusations and loud reprimands. Sit down, think the matter out, establish what you want to accomplish and then go about it in a business-like manner. This is the stuff of loyalty.

GOOD BASICS MAKE FOR GOOD HIRES

The best secret from the trenches is to hire right in the first place. This is one of the key management responsibilities and it is often neglected badly. Hiring, retaining and even firing employees can seem so complicated that owners and mangers simply fail to recognize the importance of these activities. They are focused on marketing, sales, new product development, cash flow and all of the rest of the very important management functions.

Change your perspective on this matter and do so right away. If you do not know how to hire well, it is time to learn. If you focus on the fact that you have had and do have now stable, productive employees, you soon realize that it is so much easier to have a team that performs well. Everything you do or say to improve the environment and help people who work for you is frosting on the cake.

Business Best Tip

Hiring the best job candidates means that you need to find out if the prospective employee will like and thrive under your management style. The best way to do this is by probing attitudes about former supervisors. Consider some of the following leading questions:
- Can you tell me about the best manager you ever had?
- Why was she the best?
- Who was your least favorite supervisor and why?
- How did you resolve a disagreement with a former manger?
- As a manager, what would be the most important thing for me to do to support you?

A big part of the hiring process is know who you want and why. But before you get to that, you have to think of what this person going to do. Do you have a basic job description? Just helping out in marketing is not good management and not a way to build team morale. No matter how large or small your company is, from the CEO on down, everyone in your employment needs a current job description—not one written 10 years ago.

Why are job descriptions so important? Providing a written job description to every employee, especially the ones you are about to hire, offers clear expectations about tasks and responsibilities, and will eliminate duplication and finger-pointing. In small companies where job functions often overlap, job descriptions provide clear-cut direction to each employee and serve as a benchmark for evaluations, pay increases and bonuses.

A job description typically outlines the necessary skills, training and education needed by a potential employee and lists the job responsibilities and duties. It can provide a basis for interviewing candidates, orienting a new employee and evaluating job performance. A well-designed job description simplifies the interview process and informs candidates of a job's requirements. If you know the skills you are looking for, you will have a much easier time knowing what questions to ask and identifying which candidates will best fit your open position.

Here are eight rules to follow when writing an effective job description:

1. Use clear and concise language.
2. Use non-technical language whenever possible.
3. Avoid unnecessary words.
4. Begin each sentence with an active verb.
5. Describe the desired outcome of the work.
6. Use generic terms instead of proprietary names.
7. Avoid using gender-based language.
8. Qualify whenever possible.

Descriptions of job titles appear in a variety of forms in the workplace. Recruitment ads, compensation surveys and other benchmarking tools, as well as corporate or departmental development plans, all use some method of describing a job. Get it all done at once by preparing a document for each and every position within the company.

WRITTEN EMPLOYEE POLICIES ARE A MUST

If you want to be consistent in dealing with your employees—and you should—you must make sure they understand how you expect them to conduct themselves at the workplace. The best way to do this is to create an employee policies guide or employee handbook, and make sure that your employees read it and consent to it. The guide should be a living document, and should change as circumstances require. As long as you have your expectations in writing, you and your team can refer to it in the event of an apparent violation or misunderstanding about proper company procedures and policies. Your challenge is to identify the areas the guide should address, to create a document that your employees will comprehend and to communicate to your team any changes you make to the document.

By law, some employee policies have to be in writing, such as sexual harassment. These policies can be the framework for an employee policies guide. The guide is not a legal document. It is not a contract between you and your employees, but a guideline to what you expect from your staff. Your employee manual must prominently state that it is not a legal document and should not be viewed as such.

As a rule, most employees should sign a non-compete agreement. Maintenance workers or part-time employees do not need to sign; but anyone who has significant responsibility for the day-to-day operations of your company should. Many companies make this part of the employee policies guide, but it can be a standalone document. A non-complete agreement is especially important if you run a consulting company or have a sales staff. A non-compete agreement prohibits employees from taking your clients or customers with them if they go to another business. This type of agreement is usually effective for a one-year term.

It is important to be consistent when writing your employee policies guide. There are few things more destructive to team morale than the perception that some people are given special treatment. Having an employee policies guide tells your employees that your company will treat everyone fairly. It also tells your supervisors that you will support them in enforcing employee policies, so long as it is done by-the-book in all cases.

Another important benefit of a good employee policies guide is that it helps your business avoid future lawsuits from disgruntled ex-employees. If your policies guide has been carefully reviewed and approved by a labor law attorney and you document how an employee violates the policies, you can more easily defend the actions you may have taken to deal with the violation.

Your employee policies guide will be geared towards your specific business and it will also address several areas common to most businesses:

- An introduction to the manual and a welcome to new employees;
- the company's mission statement;
- the company's history;
- the business organization (preferably using an organizational chart);
- general policies such as hours of operation, opening and closing procedures, safety procedures, smoking rules, dress code, drug and alcohol policies and the work environment;
- employment-at-will statement;
- harassment statement;
- payday, overtime and comp time policies;
- sick days, comp days and vacation days;
- maternity policy;
- company holidays; and
- a brief explanation of fringe benefits (with details in supporting documents).

Avoid the tendency to create a highly-detailed policies manual or it will be so lengthy that most employees will neither read it nor easily refer to it. Simply cover the most important points of each topic, so that your employees will not feel hemmed in by rigid guidelines. The policies included should focus on issues that affect the majority of your employees. Recognize that you cannot cover every contingency in an employee manual, no matter how lengthy it is.

If your staff creates or revises the employee manual, you must review it carefully and revise it as you see fit. Whether you create the manual by yourself or in a committee, you should always have your manual reviewed by an attorney qualified in labor laws. This will ensure that your policies are lawful and cannot be used against you by a terminated employee.

Require all employees to read the manual, and to sign and date a statement that they read the manual and understood it. This should be required of new employees soon after they are hired. Whenever you distribute a revised manual, this same process should be required of all employees. Then, if an employee later says that he or she was unaware of the policy, you can point out that the employee signed off on the statement of understanding.

It is important to avoid using the word shall in an employee policies manual. The word implies—and may be legally interpreted—that employees can choose whether to meet policy requirements. Substitute the word will, so there will be no doubt as to your intended meaning.

You may need to create more than one type of employee manual if specific policies will apply to one group of employees and not another. You can easily adapt your manual to different employee groups by housing it in a three-ring binder. You can decide which groups need what policies by constructing a simple chart, such as the one below:

Potential Handbook Topics	Full-Time	Part-Time	Seasonal	Management	All Employees	Who Develops the Policy Statement
e.g. Business Policies	X			X		

Your employees are probably a diverse population and may have different levels of literacy. You must make sure your manual is written in a clear and concise style, using simple, direct language. Make it easy to read by including enough white space on the page and between paragraphs. Include a table of contents, and put tabs in the manual so employees can easily find specific sections. In some cases, it makes good sense to translate the manual if you have a large number of non-English speakers as team members. It can be costly, but it may well be worth it in the end.

Do not put confidential company information into the manual, such as client lists, income statements or personal information about your employees. An employee may have friends or family read the manual to offer their feedback, and you do not want people outside the company learning sensitive information about your organization.

An employee policies guide should never be written in stone because the nature of business is always changing. It must be a living document, able to be amended based on new laws, changes in your business or what you have learned from previous experience. Review your manual on a regular basis, or have a management committee review it, and make any necessary changes. Distribute these changes to your employees and make sure they acknowledge in writing they have received them. If the changes are significant, you need to do more than just write them out and explain them to your team members. You need to sell them, getting everyone to understand the changes and to internalize them.

Avoid a cookie-cutter approach to your manual. Remember, the policies in it will often be specific to your company, city and state. Using another company's policies, no matter how generic they might appear, may create serious future problems for you and your business. You can purchase software programs that help you create an employee policies manual using preformatted templates. You can then print your manual, burn it to a CD-ROM or e-mail it to your employees. You can also easily add or revise your policies as often as needed.

GOOD CHEMISTRY CAN MAKE A DIFFERENCE

The best candidate to fill your job opening brings the requisite skills and experience plus a great personality. That is the perfect package. In an ideal world, you would not have to choose between an applicant with better credentials or one with whom you would enjoy good chemistry. But in reality, you may need to compromise in one of these areas. In weighing whether to hire the highest-qualified expert or an engaging, likeable candidate, think in terms of your return on investment.

You will spend 40 to 60 percent of a year's wages in developing a productive employee, says Tom Shay, a St. Petersburg, Fla.-based consultant who leads management seminars. This investment is more likely to pay off if you hire someone who is easy to bond with as well as trainable (open to learning and eager to listen and apply new skills).

Suppose you are looking for a new assistant, someone who will be a key member of your staff. You are going to promote from within and need to decide between two good employees. The experience and credentials of one outshine those of the other, but you feel more comfortable dealing with the inexperienced person. It is not that the first employee is bad or abrasive; it is just that you do not get the feeling of being on the same wavelength that you do with the second.

So do you go with your gut feeling? It is easy to be fooled by your feelings, and you cannot lightly dismiss good credentials. Then how do you decide whether this is the right time to go with your gut feeling? To gauge the extent to which you should favor good chemistry, ask yourself:

What are my reasonable expectations? The second person can probably learn the skills he lacks through on-the-job training or outside courses. The payoff will be an assistant with all the required qualifications plus the personal qualities you prefer.

Can you expect the same of the first person? If that ingredient is missing, chances are no amount of professional development training will supply it. That is why today's hiring managers adopt the mantra: Hire for attitude, train for skill.

What will happen in the long run? This key person must be someone you can trust and rely on because your choice is bound to reflect on the overall quality of your operation. If you see eye-to-eye on priorities, share a similar approach to problems, have good rapport and just generally click, your confidence in that person will grow. Then you will feel comfortable delegating responsibilities to him because you know he will handle them the same way as you would. You will have time to be more productive and creative; your assistant will have more opportunities for challenge and growth.

Observation

What will happen in adversity? When a mutual commitment exists, you have more assurance that your assistant's loyalties will be with you, should office politics or conflicts arise. A good relationship can take precedence even over offers of a more lucrative position.

What about intangibles? No doubt, at times you will require extra work from your assistant. This is where the person's sensitivity to your needs and dedication to your goals can make the difference between failure and success.

FRINGE BENEFITS AND TOP PERFORMANCE

Fringe benefits, not salary, are many times the deciding factor in a job candidate's not only accepting a position but staying with the company for the long term. Fringe benefits are part of an employee's compensation and part of your cost of doing business. To make the most of your fringe benefit package, you must carefully evaluate what you think will meet the needs of potential employees, what available benefits will be most effective and the ultimate cost of these benefits. You must also be prepared to make changes to the benefits you offer, properly communicate changes to your employees and monitor whether those benefits are meeting their needs.

Also known as perquisites (or perks), the basic definition of a fringe benefit is compensation that is separate from salary. Some companies employ a salary-sacrifice program, which means that benefits are offered in exchange for some portion of employee salaries. In order to keep team members productive and moving along smoothly, it is absolutely essential that you figure out the right combination of salary and benefits for your industry and for your locale.

Some benefits, such as insurance plans, are nontaxable, thus excluded from your gross income. Other benefits, including flexible spending accounts and retirement plans (such as 401(k) and 403(b)) can be used as a tax shelter. Fringe benefits vary widely depending on your business and how much you can afford to spend, but several categories are offered by most businesses:

- Relocation compensation and temporary housing for relocated employees (typically for senior managers or technical employees);
- group health insurance, either fully funded by the business or partially paid for by the employee;
- income protection insurance;
- retirement benefits;
- childcare compensation;
- tuition reimbursement for job-related courses;

- sick days;
- holidays;
- vacation days; and
- profit sharing/bonuses.

Fringe benefits can also vary across a company. Upper management personnel may be given discretionary benefits which are usually defined as perks. These are designed to lure good prospects to the company and reward them for the extra time, effort and travel they may need to do to perform their jobs. Perks such as the following can also be used to reward team members for exceptional job performance:

- Use of a company car;
- hotel stays;
- membership fees (health club, professional societies);
- personalized stationery;
- lunch allowances; and
- first choice of job assignments or vacation time.

You can choose to honor any holiday by giving your employees the day off. Typical company holidays include New Year's Day, Memorial Day, the Fourth of July, Labor Day, Thanksgiving (sometimes including the following day) and Christmas. Some companies allow one or two flex days off for holidays not normally honored by businesses, such as Martin Luther King Jr. Day, Presidents Day, Columbus Day and Veterans Day. Remember, if you operate a business that must be staffed on a holiday where other employees are off, you must provide the people working that day with another day off within a reasonable time period.

Some fringe benefits are expensive, either paid for in dollars (insurance, retirement plans) or by a loss in productivity (sick days, holidays, vacation days). Other benefits, while less expensive, can mean a lot to your employees. You can offer flex time so that employees can balance their work and personal lives. You can allow employees to telecommute from home by using remote network access and e-mail. You can even offer free snacks or a nice break room with games and other physical comforts (this will be a one-time-only cost as opposed to the ongoing costs of other fringe benefits). A new fringe benefit in the workplace is a concierge service, which runs basic errands for employees upon their request (such as picking up dry-cleaning or walking a dog). This benefit saves an employee time and enables him or her to concentrate more fully on the job.

If your workplace is large enough to include a cafeteria, you can subsidize their out-of-pocket cost for meals and snacks; the total would be less than what they would pay at a fast-food restaurant. However, running a cafeteria in your business will mean dealing with the health department and a variety of physical challenges.

Some companies periodically distribute pre-published discount coupon books to staff. These coupons are provided by local restaurants and entertainment venues. You must examine the discounts carefully for validity, however. If you live in an area with sports teams, you might consider purchasing season tickets that you can occasionally distribute to staff. Be creative with your fringe benefits; you may be surprised how much your team members will appreciate them.

Expect that job candidates will inquire about fringe benefits during the second or third interview. Be prepared to answer them honestly, and regard them as a way to recruit qualified people:

- What are the monthly or prepaid costs for your medical plan?
- Who is covered by the medical plan (just the employee or immediate family)?
- When are new hires eligible to receive benefits (immediately or after a probationary period)?
- Are benefits taxable?
- Am I required to use all the benefits or may I pick and choose?

In the current work environment, health insurance is one of the great motivators (or non-motivators, as the case may be) for employee productivity and morale. Many large retailers, for example, have received a great deal of criticism for not offering even basic insurance. They rely on a vast army of part-time team members and somehow feel that they cannot afford the cost of insurance, even if the employees are paying their share.

One of the most difficult choices you will face in selecting fringe benefits is choosing a health insurance plan. There are many health insurance companies and the packages they offer can vary widely. A poorly chosen health plan can be a true non-starter for many team members, especially if they are expected to pay most of the cost for themselves and their dependents. If there is any area of employee compensation that you should consider as important, it is health insurance. Buy the best you can afford. It is important to get the health insurance plans right, so consider the following:

- What expenses are covered?
- Are there deductibles or co-pays?
- Are there exclusions for preexisting conditions?
- Is a physical examination required for enrollment?

Establishing a 401(k) plan, pension plan or profit-sharing plan can be a daunting task. But they are important to morale and productivity. Few companies have traditional pension plans and most prospective and long-term employees do not expect to get employment which includes these kinds of plans. But everyone expects to have some kind of 401(k) plan, even if the company does not contribute or does not make a large contribution. Banks and insurance companies have off-the-shelf plans that are easy to administer. This is a good time to rely on your accountant, attorney and financial advisor to help you to devise a plan, while keeping in mind some basic considerations:

- What is the maximum amount of that employees can contribute to the plan?
- How much will your business match employee contributions?
- What is the vesting period?
- Are there options for partial investing?
- Will the basis of your profit-sharing plan be stock options or some form of cash reimbursement?
- Will there be a cap on profit sharing, or will it be unlimited based on a stated percentage and profitability at the end of the fiscal year?

THE RIGHT WAY TO REPLACE A LEGEND

When Christin gave a speech at Diane's retirement party, she couldn't say enough good things about her and how much she would be missed by the entire staff.

After the applause and cheers abated, Christin finished the speech by welcoming aboard Diane's successor, Dave. She told Dave how they all expecting great things from him. Cristin was also sure to let him know that he was replacing a legend in Diane and went on to describe how she was always ready with a solution when an emergency came up in one of their regional offices.

What a way to be welcomed aboard: your boss saying you are expected to do a great job following in the footsteps of a legend. Christin has set her new employee on a rocky path—a mistake many managers make. They overlook the fact that it is impossible to replace anyone. All they can do is put another person in the job.

True, the newcomer will have a different personality, perspective and approach, but that does not mean a poorer performance than his predecessor's. In fact, the newcomer may, in time, do even better if given the opportunity to develop his capabilities. You should focus on next person in the job. (NOTE: not sure if some text was dropped here, this sentence was rather abrupt and random)

To ensure that an employee who is following an irreplaceable predecessor gets this opportunity, consider these suggestions:

- Clarify your position. You need not hide your esteem for a former manager who did a top-notch job as long as you keep such remarks low-key and infrequent. What the newcomer needs is assurance that he's not going to face constant comparison to a paragon. Make it clear that Dave has your backing and will be judged on individual merit and progress.
- Spread the word. Many employees may have held Diane in high esteem and became accustomed to her way of doing things. Changes may lead to grumbling (That is not the way Diane did it!) and a reluctance to cooperate. It is up to you to indicate that was then, this is now. In short, it is a new start for everyone on your team.

- Separate past from present. Perhaps you and the former employee are good friends; just do not flaunt it around her successor. For example, a remark that begins with: "I was talking to Diane yesterday," could understandably make the newcomer uneasy. Have you been questioning Diane, discussing the old and the new? What conclusions did the two of you reach? Enjoy Diane's friendship, but keep it private and noncontroversial.

- Provide for alternatives. Most jobs change over time—a bit is added here or subtracted there. The general content of the job remains largely the same, but there is room for flexibility in the position's overall parameters. When you bring in a newcomer, why not tailor the job to make the best use of her special talents, perspective and goals? Let us say, for example, that the new employee has special writing skills; then you might want to delegate some report writing to her.

Keep in mind, too, the changing needs of the organization. You and the previous job-holder were used to doing tasks and procedures a certain way. It may be time for changes to meet overall goals more effectively.

> **Observation**
> During the first months of the newcomer's tenure, you may find yourself disagreeing with some of his methods or work plans. But unless you see signs of disaster ahead, give that person time to grow and succeed in his own way. Then you may eventually have another legendary individual on your team.

THERE ARE MANAGERS...AND THEN THERE ARE MANAGERS

Ask yourself what your employees' expectations are when it comes to hiring new managers. When filling a management position, do you hire (promote) from within or do you go outside the company to find fresh faces and new ideas (assuming that people from within do not have fresh ideas)?

First and foremost, it is essential to recognize that hiring a key manager is a daunting task. A mistake can be costly, both financially and in terms of team morale and productivity. The major challenge is to select that individual who will best fit into both the position and your company's culture. Hiring from within is a real morale booster—team members see that there is a long-term future with the company if they are productive, innovative and motivated.

Other team members will identify with the newly-minted manager: If she can do it, do can I.

No one wants to see themselves in a dead-end job, no matter how well paid they are or how good the benefits or how benign the manger is. Everyone has expectations of doing better and learning on the job and therefore are able to be promoted. If you never hire from within, you never capture the creativity or the potential you have within your company or your team.

Internal promotion means that your new manager will be more productive, sooner. The learning curve is much shorter—she knows where the coffee pot and the copier are, she knows other team members and she knows the company, its products and its customers. Further senior management also knows the new manager, her weaknesses and her abilities, and what they can do in terms of development, mentoring and training to assist her in being the best team leader possible.

Now that the case has been made for internal promotion, do remember that there are also reasons to go outside the company:

- You get fresh insights and new ways of operating that you may not have internally.
- There may not be an internal candidate with the right credentials or experience, say a senior finance executive.
- It is easy to assume that a good team member would also be a good team leader—the halo effect. (The traditional wisdom is that a good salesperson is not necessarily going to be a good sales manager.)
- It is assumed that an outsider has management experience, so that training in basic and advanced management skills will not be needed.
- Outsiders do not bring negative baggage that insiders sometimes have.
- Other team members may not want to take direction from a former team member, now their manager. This can be a tricky transition and may do more harm to morale than good.

Whatever the need, it is essential not to lock yourself into one strategy as opposed to the other. Weigh the key hiring criteria and weigh all candidates (inside and outside) for their knowledge, skills, management style, temperament and enthusiasm. Decide how much technical and managerial training each candidate will need and what you can realistically afford to spend. What value-added benefits does a candidate bring? He knows the competition, is technically very skilled, has strong sales background, etc. Finally, list the plusses and minuses of outside versus inside hiring.

2
Create a Supportive Environment

YOU CANNOT BEAT UPSCALE, UPBEAT THINKING

It is easy—especially when you have a low opinion of someone—to forget the high self-regard that virtually everyone has. In their classic book, *In Search of Excellence* (Warner Books, 1982), Thomas Peters and Robert Waterman, Jr. cite a study asking adults to rank themselves on the ability to get along with others. All the participants ranked themselves in the top 10 percent, and a full 26 percent ever-so-humbly thought they were in the top 1 percent of the population. In terms of leadership, 70 percent rated themselves in the top 25 percent. So much for humility.

Such studies leave little doubt about a deep and pervading vein of self-esteem waiting to be tapped. "The lesson that the excellent companies have to teach is that...most of their people are made to feel that they are winners," Peters and Waterman said. "Their people, by and large, make their targets and quotas because [these] are set—often by the people themselves—to allow that to happen."

The authors point to a major company that, "explicitly manages to ensure that 70-80 percent of its salespeople meet quotas, in contrast to a less successful competitor at which only 40 percent of its sales force meets its quotas in a given year. With this approach, at least 60 percent of the salespeople think of themselves as losers. Label someone a loser and they'll start acting like one."

Create a Supportive Environment

BOOST THEIR SELF-IMAGE

Dr. Kevin P. McNamee, a chiropractor and entrepreneur in Canoga Park, Calif., offers these tips to help your employees feel like winners:

- *Pick a lofty title.* Support staff usually lack fancy job titles, so they rarely feel like key contributors to the team. For lower-level employees who handle multiple tasks in several areas, give them a title that encompasses their role. Example: A receptionist who also does the insurance billing can serve as office manager.

- *Distribute business cards.* Give all your employees a set of customized business cards with their job title. Workers will feel more like executives as they proudly give their cards to friends and family. Expect to spend less than $20 for 500 cards.

- *End the day with praise.* McNamee caps each day by making the rounds among his employees, stopping to thank them for their efforts and accomplishments. You will go a long way toward making your staff feel special by recognizing some aspect of their performance that you appreciate or admire.

Attitudes and Values that Build Teamwork

1. Do not be afraid to say that you do not know something. For reasons no one can figure out, people somehow feel that they are expected to know everything. If you do not know the answer, do not bluff. Similarly, if you are at fault, say so and apologize. You do not have to make excuses—everyone knows that the dog did not eat your homework anyway, so why make it worse.

2. Do not gossip. It is hard not to sometimes, but resist the urge and as a manager, it is particularly important that you set the tone for this kind of behavior. When someone gossips, two careers are hurt—the person spoken about and the person passing along the gossip. Gossip is a waste of time and only causes bad feelings.

3. Even the owner or manager can pitch in from time to time to meet a deadline or help a customer. No task should be beneath you. Helping when help is needed makes your company competitive and really fosters teamwork in the here and now.
4. Share the credit whenever you can. This is especially true for managers. What does it hurt to say that one or two other people in the team were instrumental in getting something accomplished? And say it loudly, for all to hear. They feel great and you look like a real manager in everyone's eyes.
5. Ask for help when you need help. If you think you are in over your head, the fact is that you are in over your head. After all, is that not why you are part of a team? And do not forget to reciprocate when you see that someone else is in trouble.
6. Do not discuss money (or religion or politics, for that matter). Your salary and benefits are your business. Compensation is never—repeat never—entirely fair. Learn to live with the inevitable inequities of the system or find another job.
7. Do not burn bridges. If you do not like someone, live with it. Your personal likes and dislikes can only hurt morale, teamwork, and productivity.
8. Do not gloat. If you are right, everyone will get it. You do not have to say it out loud. There is no, I told you so, in teamwork.
9. Do not keep a grudge. Let it go; vent it at home or someplace other than work, but get over it. If you are passed over for an important assignment or a decision does not go your way, grin and bear it. Just like compensation, these are judgment calls and decisions can never be entirely objective or fair.

People tend to react positively to constructive comments. There is a major difference between correction and criticism: One is constructive; the other is destructive. Thus, *you can do better than this* elicits more of an I-will-try-again response than does *I am getting tired of your lousy work*.

If given the opportunity, people can surprise you. Even those you do not consider creative can emerge with fresh ideas when they sense you will listen to suggestions, consider new possibilities and act on and reward whatever

Business Best Observation

You will always encounter individuals who, for one reason or another, cannot or will not respond to encouragement, suggestions or possible rewards. They may lack the interest, energy or capability to do so. Simply bear in mind that they are the exception.

advances your operation. Employees withhold creativity when the organizational atmosphere says: We would not tolerate mistakes. There is no need for new ideas.

WHAT DOES TRUST HAVE TO DO WITH IT?

Almost everything has to do with trust, where a personal or business relationship is concerned. If you do not have trust, you cannot have an effective team environment. It is as simple as that. Trust is the most important value in a relationship, even though it is a mere state of mind, an interpretation, a very subjective feeling—and it is almost impossible to document or prove.

Trust allows you to take the word of your associate or subordinate on face value and without question or hesitation. Similarly, trust allows team members under your care to believe you when you direct their work, speak about their future in the company or the stability and growth of the organization itself. Blind trust is not the goal, as this is in reality a naïve child-like reaction to events that take place in the office.

Trust in a business environment is directly related to consistency; if you can predict other's behavior or work patterns because they have been consistent in the past, you develop a professional level of trust in that team member. In other words, you can count on them. Your goal, therefore, is to learn how people operate: pay attention, notice what results they consistently produce and where they get into trouble, so you can handle contingencies, mitigate risk or involve someone else. Similarly, you want to teach these same skills to subordinates and other team members; help them learn to trust each other, thus producing an effective group performance.

Trust has to be tempered with prudence. You would not trust an associate to perform a significant account function if he has no accounting experience or background. But you might trust someone to go beyond his or her typical work and performance boundaries, if he or she does so in an environment whereby you or other experienced team members mentor and direct the project. In other words, trust in management not only recognizes consistency in past work but also helps with the expansion of work skills and experience.

Finally, a trusting manager or team member is one who takes the fear and politics out of the workplace, a great relief to everyone. Fear produces uncertainty, eliminates initiative and ultimately reduces productivity. Trust expands the work environment and makes every member of the team a winner.

MANAGERS AND THE ART OF INFLUENCE

You have the job title, the promotion and the management position, but do you have the influence to actually pull it all off? The trick is to influence, in effect manage, without being top heavy or controlling. You real job is to get team members to buy in through example, a strong work ethic, knowledge and experience and most importantly all the intangibles that this book is about.

Effective managers, both up and down the food chain, influence their associates. They inspire people to do what they are supposed to do and they motivate everyone to increased productivity and profitability without tricks and without deception. Sounds easy, right?

Hardly.

First, you need to establish definable and attainable goals and then meet them. You are then perceived as a realist, someone to be trusted to do what they said they would do. Your influence increases with every successful outcome; your team respects you for not establishing impossible goals that were never in the cards in the first place.

Second, ask yourself what personal and professional tools and skills you have that will enhance your reputation and build your sphere of influence. (In some cases, it may be as shallow as your good looks.) But there are others that extend your influence up and down the work chain: good judgment, specific skills (technology, sales), leadership, communications (oral and written) and knowledge of the company and the industry.

The goal of business influence is to get the job done with the least amount of resistance and to get everyone to buy into the plan. The real trick is to influence without being overly political (there are always some politics) and overly aggressive.

A BUSY MANAGER CAN HAVE AN OPEN DOOR

Most employers want to attract hands-on managers who are accessible to their employees. Patagonia, Inc., an international retailer of outdoor gear, goes one step further. The company's job description for its store managers requires that they provide an open-door policy whereby employees are free to express their concerns and feelings without fear of retribution or ill-will.

Just as Patagonia insists that its managers be approachable and eager to listen, you can break down barriers so that workers at all levels feel comfortable talking with you.

Keep your office door open whenever possible, circulate among your team and hold frequent SIS meetings (meaning short, informal, spontaneous). Remember also to use non-threatening body language so employees will open up to you. For example: Keep your arms at your sides rather than folded across your chest, make friendly eye contact, be quiet while employees speak (do not sigh or fidget).

Consider the challenge faced by the manager who wrote: What does a busy manager do to look approachable to his staff in the face of a hectic schedule and lots going on? As second-in-command of a small state agency, I have more work than I can finish. Even so, I've been told more than once by someone I trust that I have a reputation for being stand-offish and intimidating. This is hard for me to take because I think of myself as someone inclined to help others. What can I do to change my present image into one that more closely represents the person who is really me?

Every organization has some employees who have only minimal contact with others and do not complain about this state of affairs. They have, so it would seem, arrived at their state of equilibrium. Presumably, neither they nor their employers feel they have to be approachable to do a satisfactory job.

Then why should it be any different for a manager? Because management is the art of getting things done through other people. But before you make any sudden changes or torment yourself for not being as accessible as some think you should be, consider:

- *You should not change your work style overnight.* Some people would not feel comfortable with a boss who suddenly wants to be approached, particularly when they have learned to live with a boss who does not.
- *Approachability does not equate with effectiveness.* While some managers are more approachable than others, our editors know of no studies showing that more approachable managers have more productive employees.
- *If it is not broken, do not fix it.* If your managerial style has been successful until now, it is likely to work for you in the future.

If you really want to be more approachable, begin by spending less time in your office and more time in other people's. Also, seek out others whenever the opportunity arises, especially those with whom you are not on comfortable terms. Emphasize meetings—face-to-face or on the phone—rather than over e-mail. Take advantage of chance encounters, even though they may not be in settings typically associated with a boss-employee relationship.

Business Best Observation

Once you start down the path of being more approachable, stick with it. A day or a week of enhanced access is not long enough to gauge people's responses. Give it a minimum of six months to acclimate yourself and your employees to this new style, then evaluate the outcome. Note: If you work at a location different from your employees, welcome their e-mails and respond within 24 hours to their questions and comments.

A BETTER BOSS IS AN ORGANIZED BOSS

There is no single management attribute more appreciated by team members than an organized boss. Conversely, someone who cannot find files, forgets meetings, fails to follow up or does not have time to listen and coach is universally considered the boss from hell. Fortunately, most team leaders get there because they can handle both the pressure of everyday work and the team-building demands expected of them. But there is always room for improve and there is always need to be organized and efficient.

How many times have you decided you have to get organized, without really knowing what that means or what you may have to do achieve this objective? Getting organized usually means recognizing what goals you are trying to achieve and how you hope to achieve them. This involves making a plan of action and a realistic timeline. The keys are to make your goals workable, stay within your schedule, be flexible if things do not work out as planned and change your goals as needed. These goals will drive your daily activities and help you make progress on what you want to do. They are not meant to make you feel like you have failed if you do not achieve the goals within your time schedule, but to act as a guide to planning your long- and short-term activities.

Goal setting takes time and sometimes this time may seem to take you away from more productive tasks. However, goal setting is just as important as managing day-to-day activities and should receive an appropriate amount of attention.

A goal is different than an objective. Objectives are components of a goal and should be seen as separate, measurable steps toward the end result. Daily objectives are worth establishing and should be part of achieving a larger goal. Of course, daily events may interfere with achieving an objective, but by knowing what you hope to achieve in a day beyond simply maintaining business will help keep you motivated.

If you work in a business with support employees, such as assistants, you need to communicate your daily schedule to them. This does not mean just telling them what appointments you may have, but exactly what you hope to do that day and how they can help you maintain your schedule and achieve your objectives.

Although many businesses go overboard on meetings, it is not a bad idea to have at least one weekly meeting with your key staff to learn what they need and how they are progressing on business goals. This information will help you in planning your goals and establishing a schedule to meet them.

Meeting goals and keeping to a schedule may mean you will need additional equipment, training or special supplies. You may also need to acquire new business information from books, business journals, Websites or consultants. You should plan on acquiring these resources, if needed, and budget them into your business plan.

You may become discouraged if you feel that you are not achieving your goals in a timely manner. Feeling that you have failed is counterproductive. Instead, examine why you are falling short of your goal and use that information to help you change the goal or adapt your schedule.

Obviously, if your team or the company itself encounters serious problems, you need to act on them immediately. It is vital, however, that you include some quiet time in your daily schedule, and make sure your staff knows when to give you some space. You can use this time to research, review the week's progress, or reflect on what you are doing and how you can improve. Consider starting or ending your day with this activity.

List all your anticipated daily activities in your schedule and update it at the end of each day. Remember to include:

- Objectives to meet for the day;
- employee meetings;
- phone calls to make and receive; and
- meetings with clients or outside vendors.

A good way to help you achieve your daily goals is to organize your tasks in order of importance. Assign each a number or letter (1 or A for high importance, 2 or B for medium importance, etc.), so you can concentrate on the most important tasks and defer others if you run out of time. Remember to set reasonable deadlines for your goals and objectives. Doing so will drive your schedule and help keep you focused on what you want to achieve.

Think of a goal in terms of a pyramid. The top of the pyramid represents your goal, such as increasing your business by a certain percentage over a specific amount of time. Then break this goal into smaller steps which will be your objectives. Use these objectives to create an action plan for your schedule. Intermediate goals, such as meeting quarterly income expectations or acquiring new business, can be placed in the middle part of the pyramid. Your daily, weekly or monthly objectives will be at the base of the pyramid. If you take time at the outset to plan your actions in this way, you can avoid feeling overwhelmed. Work through your objectives one at a time and you will reach your goal.

You might consider posting your goals on your office wall or on a white board, to help keep your goals in the forefront of your mind. Do not simply write down your goals and then file the list; it will soon be forgotten. When you accomplish a goal, you can cross it off your list. This action in itself will give you a sense of satisfaction and boost your confidence. Also, celebrate your success when you achieve your goal. Treat yourself to a nice lunch or dinner, a new book or CD or another small gift. Doing so will help keep you motivated in working on future goals.

Avoid setting your goals in stone, because many aspects of your business can alter the results you want. Remain flexible and you will avoid the stress of feeling that your goals are beyond your reach. Review your goals at reasonable intervals and evaluate your progress. Do not overlook external factors in planning your schedule. The overall business climate will affect your success.

Naturally, any assumptions about personal goals have to be related to the team or departmental goals as well. Your goals are not in isolate to the rest of the group. Everyone needs to be on the same page. They need to communicate across functions as to priorities and goals for the day, the week and the quarter.

Finally, block out a few moments in your day to do something that will inspire you. Read a motivational book, reflect on an inspirational quotation or enjoy a daily cartoon. This quiet time in your day is just as important as your work schedule because it will invigorate you and keep you from feeling overwhelmed.

WEATHER TOUGH TIMES AND STILL THRIVE

The scenario: The economic downturn has forced upper management to tighten its organizational belt, transfer or terminate middle managers and combine various operations. The remaining staff members are forced to share offices and assistants; raises are postponed. As they work harder and longer, the employees feel the strain and constantly worry whether their own jobs will be the next to go.

If your company is experiencing lean times, this scenario may sound familiar, and you may be feeling these pressures. When your boss is under the gun to do more with less, you in turn must require more from your employees. At the same time, you may become the target of others' accumulated frustrations. What can you do to preserve your equanimity without resorting to kicking the proverbial dog (i.e., your staff)?

For starters, assess the layout of your workplace. If too many workers are crammed into a small space, the stage is set for discord. Overcrowding has led to Dilbertization (as in *Dilbert*, the popular comic strip by Scott Adams) in which employees' loss of space and privacy has bred an uptight, uncomfortable environment—a sea of cubicles with movable partitions.

Aside from reconfiguring your office space, you can also maintain your self-control. Gauge your actions and attitudes to boost your own morale as well as others'. The way you handle yourself can mean the difference between an atmosphere of fear and blame and one of confidence and cooperation. How do you accomplish this? Consider the following simple suggestions.

Preventing desk rage

Research by Integra Realty Advisors in New York found a connection between "Dilbertized people and higher stress levels, impacting employee morale and productivity and leading to so-called desk rage," says Sean Hutchinson, the company president.

By giving workers more space to do their jobs and eliminating cube farms (employees herded into cramped cubicles), you can help them decompress during tough times.

"Where people can hear each other all the time, the potential for aggravation skyrockets," says Ellen Wayne, a professor of negotiation and conflict resolution at the University of Baltimore. "In cubicles you cannot help but listen to everyone else's conversation—automatically eavesdropping. You have no privacy if you want to discuss a disagreement with a co-worker."

Remember that everyone is in the same boat

When faced with downsizing, remember it not only affects the employees you lay off, but also those who remain on the job. You and your supervisors must recognize this and work with your existing employees to help them cope with the process. They probably will not feel grateful that they still have jobs. Rather, they may have a negative attitude about the company, because they will have to do more work. They may also sense that the business may be in trouble. To help ease the transition, make sure you and your supervisors are easily accessible throughout the downsizing process. Your remaining employees will appreciate that you are available to talk with them and are open to hearing their concerns.

Set an example.

The attitudes of higher-ups can be crucial. When the emotional climate at the top is negative, your behavior can set the tone for subordinates. Let us suppose that your boss handles stress poorly and makes what you consider unreasonable requests, such as asking you to give up a holiday or vacation or doing the work of a laid-off assistant. A response that shows tolerance for your boss's frustrations will help create an atmosphere of understanding and support, which everyone needs.

Conversely, reacting with resentment is likely to elicit an angry response and erode your relationship with your boss and eventually your employees. But if you can control your own resentment, you will set an example for your employees to do the same when circumstances require you to put stronger demands on them.

Speak clearly, listen closely.

When an organization is under stress, rumors abound and tempers run short. In such an atmosphere, clear communication with people above and below you is especially important. Clear up rumors before they grow and become unmanageable.

Avoid apologies.

You undoubtedly will have to ask more of your staff than you would normally deem fair. In this event, remember that an apologetic stance can be just as unproductive as showing resentment. Both attitudes are demotivators, and they diminish the respect you need to manage effectively.

When you have tough orders to carry out, remind your staff that everyone is under similar pressure, including you and your boss, and that it is important to act in unison to help get the company back on track to save jobs. The best way to impart this kind of news is in staff meetings rather than through impersonal e-mails or casual remarks. When you handle bad news as a team, the net effect often is to encourage people rather than to demoralize them.

Enhance your visibility.

Difficult times present an opportunity to show management that you are a team player, willing to pull your weight and make sacrifices for the organization. You can demonstrate your adaptability and versatility by taking on another function without missing a beat, covering a transferred manager's department while boosting production in your own or devising ways to keep morale high among your staff. That way the chances are much greater that management will notice your efforts and appreciate them.

Company mission

This is a time to reemphasize your company's mission, vision, values and goals. Discuss ideas for the work climate you want to have. Consider posting a good news board where employees can comment on things that are going well. You might want to create a morale committee, not only to plan parties, but also to look at creative ways to maintain and enhance morale. You can also take this time to form new teams, redistribute work fairly and look for staff who may be the new leaders in your business.

Departing employees

Treat employees whom you have or intend to lay off with dignity and openness. Let them know why this happens. Talk to employees as they prepare to leave to let them know how much you valued their work. If possible, provide a career counseling service or other networking services so that these individuals can find new jobs.

Routines

Maintain office routines as much as possible. Change can be stressful: If you keep to a regular schedule, your staff will see that you are committed to the business and do not intend to make any other radical changes. There are ways you can help employees keep the business running after downsizing, such as by using more part-time and temporary employees and contracting out services.

You will have to update your business plan, because significant changes have occurred. You might consider including what-if scenarios in your business plan if you believe there may be a need for future downsizing.

Exploring alternatives

There are other methods to downsize other than by layoffs. You can downsize through attrition. Instead of laying off employees, you simply do not replace an employee when he or she leaves the company. While this is a less painful method of downsizing, you have less control over when it happens. You might also ask for help from family members, who may work for little or no remuneration. This will save you money, but could create problems as well. You may not have as much control over a family member as an employee.

When the news gets out

You must inform your existing clients that you are downsizing, but emphasize that it will not affect your business dealings. Your clients and customers will surely learn of the change, and it is far preferable to inform others rather than to have them come to you with questions afterward.

If you run a high-profile business, you must be prepared to answer media questions regarding any downsizing. It is a common perception that downsizing means a business is in trouble; you will be asked about this. Stay positive, answer questions honestly and explain your reasoning. Make clear how downsizing will benefit your business and that you will continue to provide the same level of service to your customers.

> **Business Best Observation**
> It could also be helpful to adjust your outlook and regard the situation as temporary. You might set a date, two or three months away, when you will reassess matters and, if the crunch has not eased, see if another course is warranted. In the meantime, if the situation calls for extraordinary effort, your best bet is to respond accordingly.

USE INCENTIVES TO BOOST PRODUCTIVITY

Rod Walsh was fed up. As president of Blue Chip Inventory Service in Sherman Oaks, Calif., Walsh knew his success depended greatly on his employees showing up for work. But the nature of inventory work means employees face unpredictable hours (often overnight assignments on short notice) and low wages.

Rather than berate his workers to improve their attendance, Walsh decided to lure them with honey—or, more accurately, money. He launched a plan whereby he would drop by unannounced at a work site and give each worker an envelope with cash (from $5 to $50). Only those who were present received the surprise gift. "It did not add up to a lot of money, but it sure worked," Walsh recalls. "We never had an attendance problem after that because no one wanted to miss out on getting a little bonus just for showing up."

When you want to encourage employees to improve their work habits, the carrot works far better than the stick. Positive motivation (Do this and you will earn a reward) trumps fear (You better do this–or else!).

Consider how smart employers administer their health benefits. Because companies pay less for group insurance policies and related costs if their employees adopt healthy habits, it is in their interest to motivate workers to reduce their risk factors.

Carrots replacing sticks

A study by Hewitt Associates, a Chicago-based research and consulting firm, found that more employers are dangling incentives to employees (such as cash awards and gifts for participating in health screenings). They are less inclined to set up disincentives (such as charging higher health and life insurance premiums to smokers or paying reduced claims to drivers who weren't wearing a seat belt in a car accident).

The bottom line: Employees prefer to earn rewards for good behavior rather than face punishment for failing to meet an imposed standard.

To induce employees to work smarter and harder, today's managers are using creative incentives. For example:

- *Paid time off.* Workers with harried lives love the opportunity to enjoy a personal day without losing pay. Even half-days off can provide a much appreciated breather for your team.
- *Work from home.* Employees stressed by everything from long commutes to terrorism fears may relish the chance to stay home and work for, say, one day a week.
- *Perks.* Cash is always a nice motivator, but also think of sharing some prized possession with your employees. Examples: season tickets to a coveted sporting event, a VIP pass to attend a museum opening, a private screening of a movie.

- *Career boosts.* Invest in a promising employee's future by providing cross-training. Or introduce a stellar worker to bigwigs throughout your organization. Better yet, offer shadow days in which selected workers can choose someone in the company to follow around for a day. For instance, giving a clerk a chance to shadow a salesperson may prove a powerful career-development tool if the clerk has expressed interest in joining the sales team.

If you are going to use carrots, not sticks, to motivate your employees, realize that you do not need to guess which ones work best. Ask your staff how they would like to be rewarded or what incentive really excites them. Their answers can help you tailor rewards that will produce the maximum payoff.

IS FLEXTIME GOOD FOR BUSINESS?

As you know, and so does every team member, life is complicated. It is increasingly difficult to put in 40 to 50 hours a week at the office and still manage a marriage, a household, kids perhaps, social obligations and actually have some free time left over. One solution being tried more and more is flextime—e.g. allowing employees to start and end their days at different times. For example, a single working mother might find that it much easier to work early, having dropped the kids off at day care, but leave an hour or so before the rest of the team.

But flextime goes beyond traditional family care issues. Some team members may want time off to attend a class or even teach a class! Commuting problems in major cities such as Los Angeles, Atlanta, Houston and Chicago are now becoming notoriously long. Why not work with employees to spend less time in traffic and more time in the office or at home by changing schedules. Flextime can also be used to accommodate a whole group of workers who would like to work 30 hours a week instead of the usual full week. Everyone wins: you keep key personnel and the team members themselves have a significant lifestyle advantage.

Some companies see flextime as burdensome in terms of management and keeping track of who is where and when. A simple rule is to make sure that everyone is in the workplace for, say 6 hours a day. When they begin and end will be flexible. In this way, meetings and other important group activities can take place without interruption and without a loss of productivity.

Insist that workers keep to the same schedule each week. Allow for changes, say every quarter, but making sure that worker schedules are posted on the company Intranet. An important variation is allowing workers some flexibility to telecommute (working from home) instead of driving or commuting to the office everyday. Needless to say, you need some guarantees that workers are not taking advantage of the situation and that they can and will be productive at home. Even if telecommuting is not a weekly option to team members, it could be effective when the weather is bad or the kids are sick. Flexibility is the key and it is the most important component these days to keeping and maintaining a highly professional and motivated staff.

JOB SHARING AS AN ALTERNATIVE

While not without its problems and complications, job sharing is yet another alternative to motivating your team to top performance. Much like the need for flextime, it is motivated by very busy and complicated personal and professional lives. It is both expensive and increasing difficult to find care for children and aging parents, for example, and many individual need and want to work. Thus sharing a job with another part-time employee can be beneficial to both workers.

You as an employer gain, because it has been clearly documented that part-time workers are very productive, sometimes as productive as a full-time employee. Not all jobs can be shared nor should they; it is difficult to imagine that an senior financial manager can split her day with a similarly trained employee and have the continuity required to maintain optimal financial control.

But in many areas such as sales support, marketing, customer service, reception, and clerical staff, this concept can and does work nicely. To have a fully functional team, workers and managers need to solve the who-is-in-charge syndrome. This means that there must be clear and concise coordination between job sharers and their team leader. Shifts need to overlap and responsibilities clearly identified and assigned. In some areas, such as customer service, this is a fairly routine matter—pick up the phone and answer the problems and questions and follow up on calls from this morning.

Again posting schedules of work time on the board or on the company Intranet would be an excellent way to communicate to everyone times and

Create a Supportive Environment

Business Best Observation

Some will always favor using the stick instead of the carrot: docking pay, threatening to fire or demote someone and keeping employees in the dark about management decisions. But intimidation rarely achieves the consistently high results that encouragement does. When incentives are misused by managers, they become disincentives to employees.

schedules for individual employees. It is perfectly reasonable that in an emergency or when need arises, that the job sharer who is not at work be contacted at home or on a cell. Assuming that the calls are not every 5 minutes, most reasonable people will not object if there is sufficient justification. An e-mail to home also would work nicely in a pinch.

3
Empower Your Staff

NEWS ON TODAY'S PARTICIPATIVE SYSTEMS

In recent years, the traditional authoritarian style of management has been losing ground to the participative management systems that reward workers' input. While larger companies started the trend by introducing and developing various worker-participation strategies, smaller companies are adapting these techniques and programs to their own operations.

One such system that boosts employee participation is called needs and offers. Here is how it works:

1. A manager who wants to create a more participative work environment for her employees holds a staff meeting. She starts by asking what she needs to do better to be more effective. The manager instructs the group to spend 30 minutes developing specific answers to the question. She then adds that she is not asking them for a wish list or for a general critique of what they like or do not like about her. She wants them to focus on her effectiveness as a manager in helping everyone achieve their goals.

2. A half-hour later, the group reconvenes. After listing how they think the manager could be more effective, the employees make offers along the lines of: In return for X, we will do Y. Example: In return for you not micromanaging us, we will keep you in the loop better.

3. The group discusses the offers with the manager and tweaks them so they are acceptable to everyone. Then they write them down so there is no ambiguity about the terms of each offer.

4. In a few weeks, the group meets to evaluate to what extent both the manager and the staff are honoring each offer.

> **Business Best Observation**
>
> Employees appreciate the opportunity to contribute their knowledge to improving operations and product quality. What is more, increasing workers' responsibilities translates directly into greater job satisfaction and a heightened sense of loyalty to the company.

"Needs and offers is a great way to turn employees into participants," says Ingrid Bens, a Sarasota, Fla.-based consultant and author of *Facilitating With Ease* (Jossey-Bass, 2000). She adds that 360-degree appraisals (consisting of both peer review and giving feedback to higher-ups) have also gained popularity, along with inviting employees to participate in hiring new workers.

MANAGEMENT BY DELEGATION

Does this sound familiar? You are walking around the office, and a team member approaches and reports at length on a rather routine matter, like the copy machine needs repair. You wonder why you are in the loop on this matter at all. It is his department and he runs it, so why give you the skinny and all the details and ask what to do? This can be more than a little frustrating and more than a bit non-productive. But step back for a minute and ask why this is happening. Perhaps it is not the employee but you. Perhaps you may have not made it clear enough that you wish to delegate responsibility and you have not implemented it in your management scheme.

To change this pattern, you want to stress results, not all the details. Who needs to know the what and why of everything that goes on every day. It is a ridiculous waste of time. Start telling team members that you do not need the details, but only the outcomes. That is not an invitation to skip proper recording keeping or procedure, but rather to get to the final outcome on all projects directly.

Avoid the situation of giving the solutions to employee problems. Let them figure it out and, if necessary, report back as to what the strategy and solution is going to be. Not every event can be handled this way, but you will find an increasing number of situations where this will work nicely. Do not be afraid to turn a question around when an employee comes to you with a problem. Ask her for the solution and the strategy.

For all work, you need to establish measurable and concrete objectives so you can instill confidence in employees taking the initiative and solving problems on their own. If they can feel and touch the goals, your life will be much easier. Similarly, put in standard reporting systems, again that can be quantified, for weekly or monthly updates. Have them posted on the dashboard portion of your Intranet for everyone to see.

If you are going to delegate, you must give deadlines. None of this next-month business. Set a strict and specific target date to which the team members can work. But remember that the dates also have to be realistic. Engage the team itself in this decision; find out from them what the first possible date is for the project to be completed and hold them to it.

For your part, keep a simple log indicating that you have delegated authority for various projects to different team members. This will help you just as much as the team members. Not all team members can handle delegation management, so work carefully with those that can and train and mentor those that you feel cannot work this way.

Finally, when delegating work, you have to know your individual team members and their strengths and weaknesses. Why delegate something such as a sales analysis project to a person who does not have the math or analytical skills to complete the task? All you are asking for is frustration and setting your team member and yourself up to fail. You need to know what individuals can realistically accomplish. It might be an excellent strategy to pair team members, one experience in sales analysis and another who has the potential and motivation to learn--that mentoring thing, again. Not only do you get a particular project done on a timely basis, and correctly, but you build team strength for the future. Everyone is empowered and you take a lot of work off your desk.

WHEN YOUR STAFF SUCCEEDS, SO DO YOU

Over his long career climbing the corporate ladder, David D'Alessandro has learned to tamp his urge to micromanage employees. Today, the CEO of Boston-based John Hancock Financial Services balances his eagerness to take a hands-on role with a willingness to step back and trust workers to do their jobs. "My job now is to patiently listen, hear their various views on whether we should do this deal or that strategy and then reach a judgment," he told *The Wall Street Journal*.

D'Alessandro knows what it is like to work for a micromanager. Years ago, he reported to someone who second-guessed employees' work and forbade them from talking to anyone above him without letting him know what they discussed. "He perpetuated the myth that only he could do things right," D'Alessandro recalled.

Giving people responsibility and leaving them alone to do their jobs is something many managers would not do. For one reason or another, they handle the big jobs, all the important work themselves. Or, when they do hand over a major project, they hover over the employee, constantly rechecking, giving directions, making changes and generally running the whole show. True, the job gets done, but in the end, the manager and the employee do not gain much from the experience.

Resist the Urge to Micromanage

At times you may have noticed a similar tendency in yourself. Rather than hand over an important project and let a qualified assistant go it alone, you have added it to your own busy schedule or stayed in charge as the person struggled to get it done.

This tendency is characteristic of managers who do not realize that it is important to their own development and promotability to have a staff capable of growth and doing a larger job. Next time you find yourself unable to leave an employee alone to do a project, ask yourself:

1) What am I afraid of? Managers who are reluctant to delegate can usually come up with what they consider logical explanations for their stance: He would not be able to get it done on time. She is bound to

make some mistake. I can do it better and faster, etc. But this kind of reasoning is based on the fear of letting go, of losing control. As such, it is not realistic or practical and is certainly not helpful.

2) What have I got to lose? The answer depends, of course, on the nature and importance of the job. In some cases you might stand to lose a great deal if the job is not handled successfully, but consider this: You can give an employee a basic idea of what needs to be done, build in deadlines and stand by to provide assistance if necessary. All these safeguards will help ensure that the job gets done right and on time

3) What have I got to gain? Chances are, a great deal. For starters, you will be lifting a heavy burden off your shoulders and have more time for other projects. True, you may have some worrisome moments, but that is a small price to pay for not having to take on everything yourself.

> **Business Best Observation**
>
> Far more important, though, is the fact that you will be allowing an employee to develop and grow. In giving someone responsibility and leaving her alone to do the job, you will be making an important contribution to that person's eventual success, not to mention your own. Why? Because managers who indicate that only they can do a particular job are liable to be stuck with that responsibility permanently.

THE SEE-HOW-IT-GOES APPROACH

The flight of the human-powered Gossamer Albatross across the English Channel in 1979 was a remarkable and rather unsung feat of U.S. technology, accomplished in direct competition with teams from Japan, England and other countries. Construction of the craft involved some unusual managerial circumstances.

In his book, *Gossamer Odyssey* (Houghton Mifflin, 1981), Morton Grosser writes about how they assigned daily work on the craft:

> The construction chief, or whoever was acting foreman for the day, would go over to the airplane and write down all the jobs that needed to be done. His list, usually written on several sheets of lined yellow paper taped end-to-end, was then posted on the hangar wall. Whenever someone finished what he was working on, he would stroll over to the list and

scan it from top to bottom. Hmmm, was a common audible accompaniment to this survey, followed by, I guess I can do that. Most often, [this procedure] resulted in people's doing what they were best at and producing a successful and well-crafted plane in a remarkably short time.

YOUR OWN GOSSAMER

Despite the unique objective of the Gossamer project, every manager can learn something from its success. At some time you may become involved in a project whose previous guidelines were scanty: coming up with a market for a novel product, say, or adapting to a new energy source. When that happens, consider whether some of the approaches that worked in the Gossamer project will prove useful to you. For example:

- Can leadership be shared? What if the supervisor could assign tasks one day and the acting supervisor the next? Let necessity and circumstance, rather than a prior agenda, be the guide. Then a supervisor who becomes heavily involved in one phase of the project can pass leadership responsibility on to another team member without jeopardizing the project. Indeed, you will likely see a net gain owing to wider-ranging participation in various project phases.

- Can responsibility be shared? Each Gossamer project member had to take a periodic, even daily, look at what had been done and what was next. As a result, members tended to view the project in terms of its progress toward completion, not just from the viewpoint of their own skill or interest.

- Can project members choose their assignments? A rigid management approach would not allow this. In the Gossamer project, however, the result of this self-selection was a sorting of talent and personality that proved highly successful. When an employee undertakes an assignment and feels that he can do it successfully, he can become highly motivated, learn fast and accomplish much.

Innovation does not occur on command. A prominent American inventor, Dean Kamen, jokes that you cannot write into your daily agenda, 10 a.m.: Innovate. Kamen, who created the Segway human transporter and a wheelchair that climbs stairs, runs Deka Research and Development Corp. in Manchester, N.H. He urges managers who want to spur innovation among their employees to accept risk, failure and unpredictability as necessary elements. He also argues for taking greater risks and doing bolder experiments early in the innovative process.

"Projects should fall behind schedule sooner so there is more time to catch up," Kamen said in a speech at the InformationWeek Spring 2003 Conference in Amelia Island, Fla. That way, you have more time to recover from missteps without incurring high costs or deflating customer expectations.

Business Best Observation

For a manager, certain circumstances may call for a special approach. True, you cannot discard every management practice that is worked in the past, but you can experiment with one or two new ideas and see how it goes.

REMEMBER THE BASICS: THE IMPORTANCE OF EMPLOYEE REVIEWS

One of the most important tools in maintaining employee motivation and productivity is the employee review. It can be held annually, semi-annually, quarterly or even monthly. Whatever the schedule, the goals of the review are to identify what the employee does well, what needs improvement and what goals to set for the next review. A good employee review will also allow you or your supervisors to see how they are doing their jobs. Almost everyone in management is uncomfortable with reviews and tries to avoid them. However, if conducted in a positive light and with an eye on melding the review into the general goals of your business, the employee review can be of great benefit for all parties.

So resist the urge to procrastinate; you should view an employee evaluation as an opportunity and not a chore. You should also make every effort to explain to team members being reviewed that this is meant to be a positive process, a two-way communication and a way to help everyone better perform their jobs. Naturally, team members are as reluctant as you are--unless, of course, they know they have done a great job and the review is directly tied to an expected increase.

Most reviews are done on an annual basis, based either on the employee's hiring date or on a specific date for all employees. However, you can schedule reviews on a more frequent basis, such as semi-annually or quarterly. If an employee is having difficulty, you may want to review her on a monthly basis.

This may not be the formal review, but rather an update on specific goals and objectives that have been identified and agreed to by both parties at previous meetings. The use of frequent employee meetings is an excellent means of managing a team member who is struggling.

In theory, a review is a two-way street. This is where a lot of managers and owners get into trouble because they do not see the review as a mutual process. Rather, they take a bit of an authoritarian approach, insisting in their minds that this is an employee review, not a management review. Certainly, you want to use the review to find out how your employees are doing and what they want to do, but it is also a chance for them to tell you how you can help them do their jobs better. Open yourself to insight and suggestions from team members. They might have ideas on a personnel issue, such as acquiring new staff, or it may be a need for updated equipment. And more close to home, they may have keen insight into your management style and how it impedes the team efforts.

Recall that a major part of the review is for your employees to establish measurable goals and objectives for the next review period. Goals are long-term items, while objectives are specific steps toward achieving a goal.

It may serve your company's goals and objectives and your management style to consider some nontraditional review methods which may suit your unique business needs. Those methods include:

- Peer reviews, created and implemented by an ad-hoc committee of your employees. Peer reviews do not usually lead to raises or promotions.
- Self-reviews, which allow employees to rate themselves using a prescribed format.
- Upward assessment reviews, in which employees review their supervisors. Someone besides the supervisor being reviewed will compile the results and send them to you.
- A 360-degree review, which includes all of the preceding types of assessments. Your employees may view the 360-degree review as the most valuable .

Keep meticulous paper records of employee reviews in your human resources files. This will prove vital if you have to discipline or terminate an employee. If you terminate an employee without proper cause or notification, you could be successfully sued for wrongful discharge.

It may be tempting to rush through a review. An effective review, however, requires careful preparation:

- Review the employee's job description and make sure it is still accurate.
- Determine the performance measures that you will use for your assessments. This will help you cover the goals and objectives that the employee achieved during the previous review period.
- Do not ambush your employee in a review. Communicate any concerns you may have to the employee before the review meeting.
- Give your employee adequate time to prepare for the review.
- Meet with the employee in a dedicated space where you will not be interrupted.
- Have a written draft of the review ready when you conduct the review.
- Stay focused on the ultimate goal of the review.

You should prepare a written agenda for the review that will guide you through the process. Such an agenda would include the following steps:

1. Open with a warm greeting and general discussion.
2. Summarize the employee's performance.
3. Acknowledge accomplishments.
4. Discuss perceived weaknesses in a non-confrontational manner.
5. Ask the employee to critique his or her performance during the review period.
6. Ask whether you can do anything to help he or she perform better.
7. Discuss any increase in salary.
8. Close with a positive comment, or, if necessary, alert the employee you want to do a follow-up review in the near future.

A key review tool is the self-evaluation form. You should give this to the employee to prepare at least one week prior to the review. The form helps your employee focus on what has happened in the past review period and what goals to set for the coming review period. The form you use will depend on your type of business and, in some circumstances, the specific department in which the employee works; a self-evaluation form for a manufacturing employee probably differs from one for an office employee. Generally, however, there are several questions the form should include:

- What work did you most enjoy, and what made it enjoyable?
- What skills and talents did you acquire that helped you do a good job?
- What presented the most challenges to you?
- What results are you most proud of?
- What skills would you like to learn during the coming review period, and how do you expect them to impact your job performance?
- What new projects would you like to pursue, and how would they benefit the business?

Performance reviews often tie pay increases to a rating of employee job performance:

- Unsatisfactory: work product does not meet the minimum performance standards. Suggested pay raise: 0%.
- Below average: work product meets the minimum performance standards. Suggested pay raise: 0-1%.
- Satisfactory: work product meets the minimum performance standards. Suggested pay raise: 1-3%.
- Good: work product meets minimum performance standards, and exceeds standards in some categories. Suggested pay raise: 3-5%.
- Excellent: work product exceeds minimum performance standards in most areas. Suggested pay raise: 5-8%.
- Exceptional: work product exceeds minimum performance standards, and employee has gone above and beyond to accomplish other goals. Suggested pay raise: 8-10%, and possible promotion.

Rewarding employee performance is part of the review process. While a raise in pay or bonus will be much appreciated, there are other ways to reward employees:

- A certificate or plaque recognizing excellent performance;
- a reserved parking space;
- a handwritten thank-you note;
- a pay raise and bonus tied to other tangible rewards;
- a promotion with a better office space and more responsibility;
- company-wide recognition, perhaps a monthly lunch or breakfast where you recognize those who have excelled and why;
- extra vacation days or paid time off; and
- the opportunity to attend conferences or take outside training to further enhance their skills.

IN-SERVICE TRAINING MOTIVATES AND ENHANCES TEAM PERFORMANCE

Every team member wants to have variety in his or her assigned responsibilities and wants to stay productive and motivated by learning new skills and putting them into practice to the benefit of the team and the company. Remaining productive means being aware of the latest technologies, products and customer relations techniques. Offsite training, however, can be expensive. While your employees are not at work, your business will suffer a loss in productivity. One possible solution is to use in-service (or in-house) training, in which the trainer comes to your workplace. This approach to training has its strengths and weaknesses, so you must carefully consider what you want to accomplish during training, who you should to hire to do the job and how to evaluate the results.

There are several reasons in-house training is preferable to offsite training:

- Employees do not need to take extra time to travel to the training.
- You can easily monitor the training to make sure it stays on track.
- Employees can conduct business during breaks.
- Training can be scheduled over weeks, even months, making it easier on everyone.
- Clearly, in-house training will be less expensive, even with extras such as lunch or other goodies to enhance the team experience.

- The training program can be customized more easily to your company's or your team's needs.
- You must carefully evaluate why you are planning your training and how you hope it will benefit your business:
- Do you want to enhance general skills such as communication, morale and organization?
- Do you want to address a specific aspect of the business, which may or may not include all employees?
- Do you want to help employees adjust to upcoming changes in the company?

These criteria will help you evaluate in-house training programs to ensure they are in line with your needs:

- What type of experience does the training company or the specific trainer have?
- Has this trainer worked with similar companies or in similar situations?
- Does the trainer have verifiable proof of success with past training efforts?
- What references does the trainer have?
- What evaluation methods will the trainer provide you and your employees?
- What materials will the trainer provide?

Pre-service training is a special type of training that is held for new employees before (or shortly after) they begin working for a company. This training will likely be provided by yourself or your human resources personnel. It will cover the areas of office conduct, vacation and sick time, human resource issues and building security. You can maximize the time you spend on this type of training by following some simple rules:

- Plan the orientation carefully and use a script or careful notes. Make sure all presenters are familiar with the plan.
- Set goals for what you expect to accomplish.
- Allow plenty of time for questions and answers.

- Make sure your presenters have good training and speaking skills. A good manager may not necessarily be a good trainer.
- Promote teamwork and communication.
- Ask the participants to teach one another by sharing their previous work experience.
- Ask for feedback both during and after the training session.
- Emphasize your company's belief in advanced education as an investment.

Some employees may consider in-house training to be a waste of time and money. You must make sure your staff buys into the importance of training for the benefit of them and your company. And this is not easy. Just because you say it is so, does not obviously mean that it is going to happen. Plan and anticipate employee resistance. Meet weeks before the training is to begin and stress the importance, asking for suggestions on needs and content, and do not ignore these suggestions.

One training session may not be enough to address a specific need. Because people learn by repetition, you may want to schedule a brief follow-up session to make sure your employees understand what you have taught them. Avoid over-scheduling or your employees may think they are spending more time in meetings than working.

The success and failure of a training session, assuming that it is relevant to employee needs, is the selection of the trainer. As everyone knows, there is nothing worse for morale than a training session that goes on and on and on with a monotonous speaker. The selection process is critical, so do your homework:

- Ask colleagues to refer trainers they have used;
- search the Internet, but do so with a good deal of skepticism;
- read articles and look at advertising in industry magazines or newsletters--trainers write and speak frequently just as a means to market their services; and
- attend seminars and speak to trainers who impressed you.

If training is going to be a morale booster, it needs to actually help people do their jobs or help them enrich their jobs. A general course on communication may be nice, but a program on handling specific customer objects may be more useful and appropriate. Another way to select training–although not necessarily the trainer–is to conduct a training needs assessment. Ask your employees to tell you what they need to help them do their jobs. You can do this through a memo or e-mail, but a more effective method is through an actual meeting:

1. Gather employees with similar jobs in a conference room and have a whiteboard or flip chart available.

2. Ask each employee to write down 10 training needs and to be as specific as possible.

3. Ask the employees to read their lists and have the facilitator write their responses on the board.

4. Ask for a weighted vote to determine which has priority. Use colors or numbers to rank needs.

5. After the meeting, create a list of the most important needs as prioritized on the board.

6. Schedule another session to brainstorm the final results and narrow them down to three to five training needs.

7. Follow up on the training needs in a timely manner. Otherwise, your employees may feel their time has been wasted.

Organizing group training sessions and meetings is a bit of an art. The last thing you want is 20 people sitting in a room waiting for the show to begin. Not only is it a loss of productivity for the business, but it causes cynicism and boredom--hardly a good start to a plan that is supposed to motivate employees. Make sure your trainer tells you what equipment he or she will need (such as an overhead projector, computer projector or sound equipment), what the trainer can provide and/or what you will need to supply. Make sure the equipment is compatible with the trainer's needs and is in working condition. Have the room set up the night before.

Provide a dedicated space for the training. Make sure your employees are not pulled from the training (except for emergencies) and that no phones will ring in the room you are using. Require all employees to turn off cell phones or pagers or put them in silent ring mode. Your employees should have no work with them. Request that they pay attention and give honest feedback at the end of the training.

If you are going to conduct company-wide training, you must determine how your business will operate during that time. One way to do this is to conduct the training in shifts on different days. If that is not possible, make sure a message system is available you can check periodically, and look at your e-mail during breaks. Adapt your outgoing message or create an auto-response on your e-mail that alerts customers as to why you are temporarily unavailable, but stress you will get back to them in a timely manner.

Allow your employees to give you feedback from the training. Make sure that the trainer's evaluation form—if you use it—answers the questions you need to know. If it does not, provide a separate evaluation form. Do not make it any more complicated than necessary. Include questions such as:

- Was the training conducted in a professional and organized manner?
- Were the audio-visual aids helpful?
- Are the take-home materials useful?
- What specific knowledge did you acquire that you can use in your daily work?

AN EMPLOYEE RETREAT: HOW TO MAKE IT A SUCCESS

The daily activities of your business probably leave little time to build employee relationships. You may occasionally host in-house training events or have your employees attend outside seminars, but when was the last time you got your staff together offsite for a thorough review of what you are doing? These events are usually called retreats, and the name is fitting. A retreat allows staff to spend at least one day away from their e-mail and telephones and concentrate on what is going on with your business and how it can be improved. A retreat not only is beneficial in helping motivate employees, but it can also help boost morale. The challenge is to properly plan the location, logistics and agenda of the retreat to maximize the benefits to you, your employees and your company.

There are many important things to consider when planning a retreat:

- *Location*: Do you hold it at a nearby hotel or convention center? Do you host it in your home? The wrong location for a retreat may negate many of its benefits. Creature comforts are important in a retreat, especially when you are asking employees to spend their off-hours attending it.
- *Advance planning*: Many desirable venues are booked months in advance. You may find yourself scrambling to get a location that will suit your needs and those of your employees.
- *Length of time*: Most retreats last a couple of days, but in some cases a longer time period may be desirable. Many companies hold an entire week of events for a retreat. The time frame will depend on your goals and how the temporary shutdown of your business will affect you.
- *Transportation*: If your business is located in a large city where your employees depend on public transportation, you will have to arrange transportation to and from the retreat.
- *Who to invite*: Depending on the type of business you operate, you may not need to invite everybody--nor can you afford to have everyone attend. A small consulting company may want everyone to attend, but a larger company may concentrate on inviting management and key employees. Retreats can also be organized by team or department--but someone has to be around to cover everyday business the day(s) of the retreat.

It is essential that you provide research materials for employees to keep after the retreat. These could be magazine articles, Website materials or books. Do not wait to distribute them during the retreat, because the attendees will not have time to review them. Hand them out before the retreat so your employees will know what to expect and what you are trying to achieve.

Depending on the venue and the duration of the retreat, companies may encourage attendees to bring their families; this makes it easier for them to be away from home for a few days. The families can enjoy the recreational facilities of your venue while the attendees participate in the retreat. Naturally, the more you invite the greater the cost. Further, consider the purpose of the retreat: Is it a reward for good service, with less emphasis on a full day's program of business activities, or is it strictly business? If the latter, make it employees only.

You can certainly invite outside speakers to be involved in your retreat, but remember that your employees are your most valuable resource. Ask your people to prepare and present specific material or lead a break-out session. The more your team members are involved in the retreat, the better its chance for success.

Employees who do not attend the retreat are just as important as the ones who do. If you have to leave people behind to mind your business, make sure they receive the information from the retreat and consider rewarding them in some way for keeping the business going while you participate in this important activity. If the retreat is really something special, you may have a problem with resentment or ill feelings. Try to balance this out with activities, training or other perks for the non-attendees.

Like everything in business, timing is essential. Hold your retreat at a time that will not negatively impact your employees or your business. Avoid scheduling retreats during busy vacation times such as over holidays or during the summer. Many companies schedule retreats or the company-wide sales meetings in January or February.

Always visit the site where you plan to hold the retreat. You may be able to get an impression of what the site has to offer by visiting a Website or by reviewing promotional materials, but these tools are not the same as actually walking through the site and getting a feel for it.

To have a successful retreat, it is important to set achievable goals. Before you put time and effort in your retreat planning, you must know what you hope the retreat will accomplish, such as:

- Building morale;
- building teams;
- setting goals;
- strategic planning; and/or
- launching a new product or service.

Although it will add to the cost of your retreat, you should consider using a professional facilitator. This person will help you set goals, plan your agenda and lead many of the retreat events. You will then be free to actively participate in the retreat and engage with the attendees.

Remember to include social activities. You are asking the attendees to participate over and above their normal duties, and you should reward them accordingly. Consider activities such as a golf outing, a concert, a museum field trip or scheduling nice dinners.

Many retreats also include physical activities that facilitate teambuilding, such as hikes, challenge courses or even whitewater rafting. Make these activities voluntary; forcing employees to participate when they are uncomfortable will not make for a productive retreat.

Keep these things in mind when you plan your retreat schedule:

- Do not overload attendees with activities. Fatigue can set in quickly when people feel overwhelmed.
- Hold the most important activities in the morning. Most people are at their most productive in the early part of the day. Save the afternoon for lighter sessions or rest periods.
- Schedule breaks as often as possible. Even a 15-minute break will help keep the attendees alert.
- Appoint someone from your company as an administrative liaison. This person will be reachable by phone and will be able to handle any business issues that arise during the retreat.

Plan to make the last session a retreat wrap-up. List what you believe are the key conclusions that were made or how the goals of the retreat were met. Do not just let people leave without this final session.

Ask for feedback from your attendees and emphasize that you want honest responses. You may not like everything you hear, but remember that this is a constructive step. Feedback—both positive and negative—will help you determine what you did right or wrong and how you can improve future retreats.

A SOCIABLE TEAM

The challenges of the modern workplace involve more than just showing up on time and doing your job. Productivity and success in business also depends on every effort to improve employee morale and the perception that everyone works together on a common goal. Company-sponsored social activities enable employees to interact and get to know each other outside of the business environment. Employees have their own friends, family and social activities outside of the workplace, and some may not feel the need to have their coworkers be their friends. But a few simple social activities, however, can at least help them know that they are more than just cogs in a wheel. They may even enjoy developing a closer relationship with their coworkers. The challenges are in selecting the proper events, planning them for the best effect and avoiding some of the common pitfalls in employee social activities.

Social activities for your employees can take many forms, depending on your business and your staff, but they usually fall into several broad categories:

- traditional office parties, usually held around the holidays
- parties for birthdays or significant events in an employee's life, such as a wedding or birth of a child
- special lunches where the food is brought in from the outside
- summer picnics
- after work get-togethers at a local restaurant

A bit of sensitivity goes a long way. When you plan an end-of-the-year party, remember that not everyone is of the same faith. Be sure to keep in mind the diversity of your workplace and, if possible, acknowledge and celebrate that diversity during the holidays. Similarly, remember that not everybody eats meat. If you are planning an event at which food will be served, include vegetarian selections.

And then there is booze. Inappropriate behaviors precipitated by alcohol that were once tolerated are now socially unacceptable, especially in the work environment. Most office parties, whether during office hours or after work, should limit alcohol. If you do decide to serve alcohol, make sure there are alternatives available such as sparkling juice, soda or water. Also, provide your employees with an alternative method of transportation home from the party. You might consider having a designated driver or provide cab service at company expense.

A party planner can help you organize a successful social activity either inside or outside the office. Planners create menus, decorate venues and choose appropriate music. If you have enough employees, you might consider forming a Social Committee to plan the activity. It will free you up from the planning and help your employees buy into the process. Of course, make sure that the committee gets your final approval.

Sometimes it is not necessary to plan social activities for your employees. A separate room stocked with free snacks, sodas and water or a recreational activity such as a pool table or pinball machine, can encourage employees to socialize and bond.

If you are planning a social activity outside normal working hours, do not make attendance mandatory. Many employees will welcome the opportunity to socialize, but some may resent having to spend their own time with people they see every day. Not everybody is necessarily inclined to participate. Some employees have substantial commitments such as older parents or small children. Also, team members who commute a long distance may find it difficult to stay around and still get home at a reasonable hour.

A social activity can also be an opportunity for volunteer work, such as repainting a house or participating in a fund-raising walk/run event. Your employees will not only have a chance to socialize, but can feel good about what they have done for their community.

You do not have to spend a lot of money on an event. Bringing pizzas to the office for an extended Friday lunch will not cost much. The cost will be well worth it when you see your employees relaxing, talking and laughing with each other. Avoid cutting costs on a special event, however. Employees can tell when their employers save money at the expense of enjoyment.

Depending on the event, you could include your employees' families. Family-friendly events include picnics, holiday parties or special outings. Employees whose families cannot attend will nevertheless appreciate that you invited them.

Choosing what type of music to have at a social activity can be important. After all, not everybody likes jazz, rap or rock. Consider an inoffensive genre such as golden oldies or big band. Remember to keep the volume to a manageable level so people do not have to shout at each other to be heard.

Encourage your employees to not just talk business at a social activity. They have plenty of time to discuss business during their normal day. Encourage them to relax and talk about themselves. If appropriate, take a little time at the beginning of the event to ask employees to share something about themselves, such as:

- What are your hobbies?
- What type of music, books or movies do you like?
- What sport teams do you follow?
- Where did you go to school?

4
Provide Direction and Discipline

THE RIGHT PATH TO STRAIGHT ANSWERS

You know from experience that being able to count on a straight answer from your boss makes your own job easier. Yet, for a variety of reasons, you may not think that you are as decisive in responding to your own staff.

You may think a straight answer must always be a clear-cut yes or no. But a straight answer can also be an explanation of what your staff needs to do before you can finalize a decision. Below you will learn how to give solid answers without boxing yourself in.

When you need time to weigh the consequences

When staff members want something out of the ordinary, they do not always consider that it might be setting a precedent or be disruptive. Yet such considerations are vital and may require further thought.

Tell the person about your concerns. She might have anticipated them and have information that will help. If you have to do more research, tell the person what you need to find out and when you will have a decision. Then keep your promise. When you need to discuss it with your boss or another manager NOTE, this is a fragment statement, is there missing text? Too hasty a decision can get you into trouble. Cover all the bases and discuss contingencies.

Tell the person that you will have to consult with others. Promise to let her know when you have done so by setting a date, if possible.

When saying yes right away could make you seem an easy mark

You know right away that you will agree to the request, so there is no need to delay your answer. You do not, however, want to open the floodgates for more requests later.

Say yes while setting limits. For example, if an employee asks to come in late because it is the last day to get her car inspected before the deadline, you might say: Yes, if you are really up against the deadline. But we absolutely need you here for the 10 a.m. meeting. And in the future, please try to handle this kind of activity outside work hours.

When an outright no seems harsh

Your answer is going to be no, but you want to say so in a way that lets the person down gradually. If you stall, though, you might falsely raise his expectation that you will say yes. Then when you finally do say no, you could have a worse situation on your hands.

Say no but explain the reason as in, I simply cannot grant your request for another employee in your unit this year. The budget does not have any slack.

When the request is vague

Do you think I might get some assistance soon? This vague question could be answered with something equally vague. Luckily, you need not resort to this tactic. Instead, ask questions in return. What assistance do you need? Let the employee know what further information you need to answer the question in a logical way.

You can usually exert leadership by giving straight answers. But the best way to answer some questions is with a question, says Eric Vines, who facilitates CEO retreats for The Edward Lowe Foundation in Cassopolis, Mich. Vines teaches executives that withholding answers can work to their advantage, especially if they want employees struggling with a problem to articulate a solution on their own.

If an employee asks you, what he or she should I do about this difficult supplier, you could dish out a prescriptive, do-this/do-that answer. But that makes it hard for the individual to learn. It is smarter to ask questions such as: What exactly is the problem with this supplier? What have you tried so far? What progress have you made? By guiding the employee to come up with solid answers, you increase the odds the message will sink in.

Business Best Observation

When a staff member asks you a question, show that you treat it seriously. Either give a thoughtful, direct answer, or invest time in guiding the person to discover the answer for herself.

DO NOT TOY WITH YOUR AUTHORITY

From the day Susan was hired, she worked diligently. But after a few weeks, her boss told her: You have done good work so far, but next week, no more Mr. Nice Guy. Susan was confused and worried that she was not qualified for the job. As it turned out, her boss was impressed with her work and had just been playing games with her.

Something is wrong when a boss toys with an employee's security that way. Ultimately, people will no longer apply themselves or take advice from a manager who demonstrates this kind of insensitivity. Even though you wield the authority to crack jokes at employees' expense or otherwise embarrass them for the sake of some cheap laughs, your attempt to poke fun at people can backfire.

Consider the true story of what happened to Jane, an employee who intended to e-mail a short love note to her husband, who worked in another division of the same company. Jane accidentally sent the e-mail to her boss, who as a joke forwarded it to dozens of employees. Jane was mortified, not amused.

This kind of incident is all too common. A study by the ePolicy Institute found that 27 percent of Fortune 500 companies have faced sexual harassment claims stemming from misuse of corporate e-mail. As in Jane's case, many of those suits were triggered by a manager's warped sense of humor that led to inappropriate actions.

NOT SO FUNNY, AFTER ALL

As a manager, you want your employees to remain receptive to your direction, so keep in mind:

- Your words and actions are magnified by your authority. Most of your actions will seem more important to your employees than you intended. Mere teasing on your part could be dangerously distorted by your staff.
- Your humor can have after-effects. When a peer makes fun of you, puts you down or says something embarrassingly off-color, you have recourse. You can reply in kind or say you have had enough. It is harder to do this with your boss, especially when (as with Susan) you think your manager has all the power and you have none. So you say nothing and appear to be a good sport. But later you may have plenty to communicate to others, and it can have a negative effect on their attitude and subsequent performance.
- There is no substitute for seriousness of purpose. Laughter has its place, but it does not replace the kind of managerial intensity that can ignite a staff. Too often, it can have the opposite effect: making extra effort and dedication seem a bit silly.

> **Business Best Observation**
> It is hard to be anyone but yourself when you manage people. If you are given to humor and teasing, so be it. It is best to manage in the most natural style possible. But it pays to remember that what works for you among peers may not be appropriate with employees.

STAFF SHOULD ACT AS YOUR AGENTS

Generally, managers who insist on having their orders carried out in exact, literal fashion and who do not empower their staff are the types most likely to say things such as: I have to do it all or I have to be here all the time.

Such managers also are often the target of what one management expert calls malicious obedience. Staff members who resent being treated as brainless will implement orders that they know will cause damage or trouble.

What is the remedy? Obviously, the remedy lies in having employees who can act sensibly whether you are there or not and a staff willing and able to act on your behalf even when you are in error. This section explores some ways to develop this kind of relationship.

State your expectations

Do not assume that your staff (particularly new hires) will know what attitude you want them to have. Thus you might say: Eileen, when I am in a hurry or have something else on my mind, I might ask you to do something I really did not mean. I would appreciate it if you would ask me or whoever else is available about it because I might be making a horrendous mistake and need to change things around…okay?

Admit your limitations

Assure your aides that you do not claim to have all the answers. Drea Zigarmi, who writes books on leadership, suggests that you look for opportunities to tell your employees: You know, I do not think I know how to do this as well as you do. Can you help me?

Listen to objections

If you want an employee to correct you when the need arises (and it will), make your reaction positive. This may take some self-control, but the benefits are worth it.

No matter how irritated you are at having a decision questioned, it is possible to thank the person who said: It seems to me that shipping that large quantity seems risky in this kind of credit situation. Cannot we hold off for a day or two and check a little further?

Or you might thank the administrative professional who deliberately delayed typing your peppery reply to a complaining customer so you would have time to reconsider and write a more diplomatic response.

Share your thoughts

Your assistants should know on what standards your judgments are based so they can spot your inconsistencies. They should also know whether they have done right or wrong when acting on your behalf. Make it clear when you agree or disagree with their judgment.

LIGHTEN UP ON THE REINS

Business Best Observation

While it is great to get good assistance, this does not mean you should solicit your staff's approval before making a decision. After all, running the operation is your responsibility. But if you share your thoughts with them, they are likely to do the same with you. This will lead to better decisions and fewer mistakes.

Even if you think you need greater control over your operation, proceed slowly. Heed the lesson of Microsoft Corp., whose success over the last two decades is largely a result of its corporate culture. At Microsoft, bureaucracy equals defeat and employees can do their jobs without going through needless hurdles.

As David Thielen, a former Microsoft employee, writes in his book, *The 12 Simple Secrets of Microsoft Management* (McGraw-Hill, 1999), the company strives to cut any unnecessary red tape that threatens efficiency. Executives enact limited controls, but they also treat employee complaints about bureaucracy seriously.

Although you must have some control over your organization, do not make the same mistake a Chicago manager did. He initiated an elaborate system to see if his lower-level managers were following orders. Some months later, it occurred to him that while they were working harder than ever to get out the reports he requested, overall they were accomplishing less. He also realized that his own productivity had declined, and his system produced the opposite of what he had intended.

HOW IT BACKFIRES

To many managers, control means requiring approval before allowing important activities to proceed. Unfortunately, this belief has caused many operations to languish. Here is what can go wrong:

- You may spend more on the effort to control than you can possibly get in return. A new manager, faced with a request from one unit is supervisor for a costly microcomputer, acknowledged that the equipment seemed a promising solution to some serious problems in the unit. Nevertheless, he still asked for a detailed justification of the request. Between the work involved in preparing the report, answering questions, getting more information and holding meetings to thrash out uncertainties, the cost of staff time exceeded the price of the equipment, and the problems continued unabated for months.

- You may wind up getting more information than you can handle. Then you face the uneasy choice of spending your time reading reports or laying them aside even though your subordinates have gone to great trouble to prepare the reports and expect a reaction from you.

- You may assume that it is enough to institute controls, even though you need more than controls to get results. You may have overlooked sensible, corrective action. One motor fleet manager complains about how his boss flies into a rage when he reports more than three trucks out of service. But the problem is the age of the trucks and the number of mechanics needed to work on them. Because no one wants to do anything about this, the situation will be no better when the next report is due.

- You may not get accurate information if staff members are uneasy about how you will use it. Even reasonably honest people would not bring any rope if they think you may hang them with it.

- For example: A new manager responsible for investigating insurance claims used an ingenious method to show that her office had few problems with backlogged claims. She simply counted as backlogs only those cases that she had not yet assigned to investigators. Thus, several hundred cases, which still were not closed nine months later, never showed in the count and kept her records looking good.

- You may be getting information that you no longer need. Many managers feel reassured that their authority is still intact when they continue to receive reams of irrelevant information. They overlook the effort wasted in assembling it and sending it--effort better spent elsewhere.

In sum, although you must have control over your operation, too much can be unhealthy. It can stifle employee initiative, breed resistance, take more staff time (and yours) than you can justify and cost more than it saves.

So, how can you exercise controls effectively? Some suggestions:

- Keep it simple. Do not ask for more information than you can digest or your staff can readily provide.

- Only control what needs controlling. The saying, if it ain't broke, do not fix it, may be extreme, especially for managers who believe in preventive maintenance, but it contains much wisdom. Because you cannot control everything, choose those factors that make a significant difference to the health of your organization; areas where, without controls, something serious might go wrong.
- Think carefully whether your means of control helps or hurts. If your approval is needed for every initiative but you are too busy to attend to each one, you become a bottleneck.
- Explain the purpose. Employees will be more cooperative if they know how you intend to use the information requested. At the same time, they can let you know how the controls are affecting their work.
- Let assistants control what they can. Your assistants are closer to the details of their operation than you are and thus in a position to spot problems and handle them. You are the beneficiary when they know it is their job, not just yours, to note when quality is slipping, deadlines are not being met or costs are excessive.
- Consider whether your actions do not jibe with the controls you set. One manager regularly kept staffers cooling their heels in his outer office for a half hour before he began meetings. At the same time, he insisted that they strictly enforce the policy of making their own employees return from lunch promptly because "time is money." It is hard to convince people that you mean what you say if your actions are not consistent with your policy.

> **Business Best Observation**
>
> Management thinking on the subject of controls has swung in several directions over time. It has ranged from the view that controls mean constant observation and elaborate report systems, to the notion that subordinates need direction and help much more than they need controls. Today's more realistic idea is to use controls only when necessary and only with certain types of people. In other words, as seldom as possible.

HEAVY HAND OFTEN MISSES THE MARK

If you want employees to follow the rules, give them a chance to demonstrate their compliance, advises Harry J. Friedman, who runs a retail consulting and training firm in Golden, Colo. Friedman calls this process the show-me step.

For example, if you want employees to greet customers with warmth and enthusiasm, do not just tell them what to say and threaten to punish them if they fail to follow through. Instead, stage role playing and give constructive critiques so everyone will be comfortable applying the rules.

"Show me means having your staff physically prove, or show you, that they know how to perform the task at hand," Friedman writes in his retail newsletter, *On the Floor*. Otherwise, he warns, you can fall victim to bobbing head syndrome, whereby workers signal their understanding, only to ignore your rules.

Experienced managers know that administering heavy-handed disciplinary measures can be counterproductive. The supervisor who makes the most noise about lateness, for example, is not necessarily the one whose staff has the best on-time record. When every absence requires a note from a doctor, absenteeism does not always decline. Telephone courtesy is not always the best under the direction of a supervisor who habitually listens in on calls.

UNINTENDED CONSEQUENCES

One explanation for such seemingly paradoxical behavior is that extreme disciplinary measures can have the unintended effect of making employees feel less accountable for coworkers who may be breaking rules. Too much pressure from a supervisor may discourage them from exerting peer pressure. One study of employee theft, for example, found that in many operations where security measures were not strict or enforced, employees themselves discouraged coworkers from stealing.

As such, it might be a good idea to look into how workers observe the rules in your organization. Perhaps your frontline supervisors could benefit from these suggestions:

- *Make your policy clear.* Unless supervisors believe that the organization cares about clarity, they would not have a compelling reason to ensure that disciplinary matters are understood. Most of the companies showing the lowest theft rates in the study cited above had clearly defined policies. Standards of punctuality, attendance and other work prerequisites should be spelled out rather than assumed.

- Have supervisors explain the rules. To be most effective, reminders about the rules should come to the employees from their direct

Provide Direction and Discipline

Business Best Observation

If there is some disciplinary rule that your supervisors are not regularly enforcing, maybe the problem is the rule itself. Discuss with your supervisors which rules are realistic to enforce and which ones need to be changed.

supervisors and include the reasons behind them: the high costs of inventory losses, for example, overtime necessitated by undue absenteeism or the burden that latecomers put on coworkers.

- Encourage employee cooperation. The supervisor who shares mutual trust with her staff is the one most likely to inspire peer pressure among them to observe good organizational behavior. The supervisor who does everything by edict likely will have trouble in this respect.

- Enforce rules evenly. Supervisors must enforce the rules without exception to garner people's respect for them. As for penalties, the theft study also found that even relatively mild punishment was a strong deterrent but only when administered consistently.

WHEN WORKERS SPAR, WAIT TO REFEREE

Ann Taylor could not stand it any longer. As head of Houston-based Paradigm Communications, Inc., she managed two employees who always squabbled and simply could not get along. Taylor wisely waited to see if, in time, they would settle their differences on their own.

Only after it became clear that their conflict would not die down did Taylor decide to intervene. She met with the employees together and asked them to do two things: take turns stating their own case and then repeating the gist of each other's problems to confirm understanding.

"I ended the meeting by telling them they were responsible for coming up with a solution," Taylor says. "As a result, they started to work together and get along without affecting the rest of the office."

Taylor's brief but focused intervention had a happy ending because she waited for the right moment rather than rushing to referee at the first sign of discord.

LOOK BEFORE YOU LEAP

It is much the same as the delay tactic used by professional hockey referees, who often allow the players to fight. Usually, the referees step in and separate the combatants only after they have hit each other a few times. Hockey aficionados explain their behavior this way: If referees intervened immediately, they would dampen the excitement and likely receive the blows meant for the combatants. By letting the players go at each other, the referees are looking out for themselves.

Forbearance of this sort makes a good deal of sense, both for business managers and hockey referees. As Taylor recalled, "I did not want to get involved as soon as my employees started arguing. I wanted them to try to work it out without me."

So, if you are on the edge of a combat zone in your organization and have the authority or inclination to intervene, you might want to step back and consider:

- Can I benefit by holding back? Two of your staff members have a long history of disagreeing with each other, but at the same time, they are valued employees. Occasionally, in the course of a meeting, their ill will raise the temperature in the room. You could, of course, step in immediately with, "That is enough of that, you two." Chances are, they will stop, but at what cost? They may feel that they cannot express themselves openly and that you are the kind of boss who demands amity and agreement. In addition, everyone might be missing out on the kind of excitement that could make the rest of the meeting more productive.
- Can you learn more than you otherwise would? Combat has a way of bringing out, if not the truth, then certainly what the combatants believe is the truth. You may, for instance, learn of a long-standing grievance you weren't aware of or an operational error that had been kept undercover. Such information has a way of not being shared with the boss, even when it could be helpful for you to know.
- Can those involved straighten it out on their own? Sometimes it takes a fight to bring about a more amicable relationship. People who have drifted into mutual dislike and no longer communicate may begin to feel some warmth toward each other after an honest battle.

Will you be in the middle? Everybody knows what can happen when you step into the middle of a fight: The combatants may turn on the supposed peacemaker. Let us imagine that you have just joined a taskforce or a similar group whose members tend to indulge in rancorous yet productive discussion. If this is their style and it works, you would do well not to meddle.

BEWARE OF THE TEAM MEMBER WHO TAKES ON TOO MUCH

Business Best Observation

On the whole, fights are not helpful. Too often, they leave residual bad feelings and mutual distastes that are harmful to everyone. Nonetheless, combat is a part of human nature and can have a positive side. Those managers who realize this usually have more understanding and tolerance of the way people in organizations function, even when they are combative.

As recommended in this book you have delegated as much as you can, thereby enriching team members' jobs and helping you generally remove the clutter from your desk and \placing work and assignments at their appropriate level. In doing so, you find one or two eager beavers who are willing to take on everything and anything that you offer them. And, of course, these same team members are your favorite workers at first glance. On second glance, you realize that the work is not necessarily being completed or up to standards and not necessarily on time either. These team members want to help; they want your approval and they want to shine; but they take on more than they can reasonably accomplish (this is why keeping a record of your delegating is so important).

Once you begin to recognize the pattern, it is time to adjust your management style (in line with many of the concepts discussed already):

1. Tell your team you want people to say what is on their mind and to tell the truth, not just say yes. Urge them to express reservations about their ability take on further delegated work. Make it clear that they can ask for help, they are empowered to point out problems and than speaking up is good for the team, good for the manager and ultimately good for the company.

2. Look for signs of humor, jokes or exaggeration as a means to deflect the realities of the work place. Take extra time to get to know employees; watch them as they interact with other team members. Most of all, listen carefully for signs of discontent for other workers. They know that in reality an employee might takes on everything and complete nothing.

3. If the eager beaver says yes again or volunteers without even being asked, dig deeper and ask for specifics on how something is going to be organized, who is going to assist and when it will be done. And, again, write it all down. Challenge them on their assumptions about the amount of time needed and the process to complete the work. Let them know that you know that they are getting far over their heads and that they can and should sometimes say no.

5
Overcome Obstacles

NO NEED TO CONCEAL ADVERSITY

After more than 20 years of research, Paul Stoltz concluded that top-performing managers handle adversity effectively and thus tend to prevail when faced with setbacks. Stoltz, author of *Adversity Quotient at Work* (HarperBusiness, 2000), divides workers into three groups: quitters, campers and climbers. Quitters succumb to adversity campers cling to the status quo and climbers embrace challenges and conquer obstacles.

For Stoltz, climbers adapt well to change and produce better results in part because they confront adversity head-on. They seek advice, listen attentively and build alliances that strengthen and sustain them.

Stoltz and his research team at PEAK Learning, Inc., a consulting firm, have found that individuals face an average of 23 adversities per day, from worries about layoffs and terrorism to getting a speeding ticket. Some people respond by internalizing everything.

For example, managers who are struggling with problems may keep everything to themselves. No matter how harassed they feel, they may go around with poker faces. Question them about how things are going, and almost invariably they answer, that everything is fine. They may eventually solve their problems but often do not get all the credit they deserve. Because of their silence, nobody realizes the depth and complexity of what they have had to deal with.

Such managers might regard themselves as stoic, but in fact their determination to keep their adversities to themselves can work against them. Talk openly about your concerns. If you want to establish strong relationships with your peers and staff, it is better to talk about your concerns in a positive way. You will gain these benefits:

- Helpful suggestions and ideas and advice on how to deal with one or more aspects of the problem.
- Support from those who really understand what is going on.
- Applause when the solution finally takes effect.

If you decide to follow this course, however, keep in mind certain caveats:

- Be selective about the problems you discuss. Lee Iacocca, former chairman of Chrysler Corp., chose not to talk about the fact that he did not like one of his new associates or about the trouble the automaker was having with a certain wheel bearing. Rather, he talked about such problems as the need to raise money and gain concessions from the unions.
- Use the same tactics and be selective. Generally, it is the serious problems that require the most assistance. But do not completely overlook small matters; sometimes, a five-minute talk may clear up a hitch that has bothered you for months.
- Go to those in trouble. Do not hesitate to approach people who may well have problems of their own. As Iacocca said, "Misery loves company." Discussing your own problem may bring someone welcome relief from his own and could lead to a solution for both parties.
- Send out progress reports. You may not be able to appear on television as Iacocca did to tout Chrysler's progress, but you can keep people up to date on how you are doing. By keeping them informed, you may gain additional assistance in a particular area. More importantly, you will be showing them that you are in charge and working hard to reach the final solution.

- Share the applause. No matter how many people you talked to, nor how much they helped, it will be your time and effort that finally put all the pieces together. This could tempt you to take a star turn. Do not. Instead, give credit where it is due.

> **NIBM Observation**
> Action, not a stiff upper lip, is what works these days. Confidence is built on openness, not concealment.

Personally thank everyone who helped you, even in the smallest way. The next time around, they will listen to you even more closely.

Attitudes and Values that Build Teamwork

The best and most important rule to remember when trying to foster teamwork is getting everyone, and that includes the boss, to play nicely in the sand box. After literally interviewing hundreds of managers, one researcher was able to cull their advice into nine simple rules of how to behave and work with other employees:

1. **Do not be afraid to say that you do not know something.**
   For reasons no one can figure out, people somehow feel that they are expected to know everything. If you do not know the answer, do not bluff. Similarly, if you are at fault, say so and apologize. You do not have to make excuses–everyone knows that the dog did not eat your homework anyway, so why make it worse!

2. **Do not gossip.**
   It is hard not to sometimes, but resist the urge. A manager, it is particularly important that you set the tone for this kind of behavior. When someone gossips, two careers are hurt–the person spoken about and the person passing along the gossip. Gossip is a waste of time and only causes bad feelings.

3. **Even the owner or manager can pitch in from time to time to meet a deadline or help a customer.** No task should be beneath you. Helping when help is needed makes your company competitive and really fosters teamwork in the here and now.

4. **Share the credit whenever you can.**
   This is especially true for managers. What does it hurt to say that one or two other people in the team were instrumental in getting something accomplished. And say it loudly, for all to hear. They feel great and you look like a real manager in everyone's eyes.

5. **Ask for help when you need help.**
   If you think you are in over your head, the fact is that you are in over your head. After all, is that not why you are part of a team? And do not forget to reciprocate when you see that someone else is in trouble.

6. **Do not discuss money** (or religion or politics, for that matter). Your salary and benefits are your business. Compensation is never, repeat never, entirely fair. Learn to live with the inevitable inequities of the system or find another job.

7. **Do not burn bridges.** If you do not like someone, live with it.
   Your personal likes and dislikes can only hurt morale, teamwork and productivity.

8. **Do not gloat.** If you are right, everyone will get it. You do not have to say it out loud. There is no, I told you so–in teamwork.

9. **Do not keep a grudge.** Let it go; if something does not go your way, vent it at home or someplace other than work, but get over it. If you are passed over for an important assignment or a decision does not go your way, grin and bear it. Just like compensation, these are judgment calls and decisions can never be entirely objective or fair.

YOU NEED TO HEAR BAD NEWS

Henry Schacht wanted to uncover the extent to which his company's financial reporting was faulty while warning employees that cooking the books would not be tolerated. So the CEO of troubled Lucent Technologies, Inc. convened about 50 of his senior managers in late 2000 and told them that Lucent had moved uncomfortably close to the edge of respectable behavior in its sales and accounting practices, according to *The Wall Street Journal* (Nov. 20, 2002). He sought to learn more about what went wrong and how it could be repaired.

When Schacht added that there had been a breakdown in the basic processes of the company, he indirectly blamed his managers for letting it happen. That wound up muzzling them instead of convincing them to open up about what they knew.

Schacht's harsh speech left him more isolated than ever. His freshly scolded managers weren't motivated to level with him; as a result, the problems only worsened. Plagued by questionable accounting, Lucent reported a $16.2 billion net loss for fiscal 2001. Schacht stepped down as CEO in January, 2002.

ENCOURAGE STAFF TO OPEN UP

Learn from Schacht's misstep. To fix what is broken in your unit or to improve on what is already working, you need to accurately diagnose the current situation. The best way to do that is to encourage your staff to keep you informed of relevant news: the good, the bad and the ugly. Lashing out at them would not persuade them to keep you fully informed. When employees feel comfortable conveying bad news to you (and they know you would not shoot the messenger), you will gather the most honest, useful information to solve problems.

Simply telling your key employees that you want to hear the bad news along with the good is rare enough. They need reassurance that they would not be the victims of what a political commentator has called the George Ball Syndrome. (As undersecretary of state, Ball was allegedly fired by President Lyndon Johnson after telling the president that the United States could not win the war in Vietnam.) Unless your behavior indicates that you can handle negative information with fairness and equanimity, your employees are not likely to tell you about it. As the boss, your good will is too important to risk unless you actually prove that no risk is involved.

Overcome Obstacles

With this in mind, here is how you might go about encouraging the delivery of bad news:

- Make it easy for employees to see you. The manager who acts remote and seems approachable only on the proper occasion is not going to hear any day-to-day details of an operation unless the news is positive. Employees tend to bury anything negative until it can be quietly fixed. It is not so much that they do not think you can handle such information; rather, they think you want to be shielded from its effect so you can concentrate on other, supposedly more important matters. If you do not want this filter to operate, make sure you are accessible to the staff.
- Ask the right questions. You probably would not find out what is wrong by asking: How are things going? All you are likely to get is an optimistic, uninformative answer. Instead, ask a question that deals with specifics, such as, asking how a new assistant working out or if the new modifications are as helpful as you thought they would be. Questions such as these convey the idea that you are familiar enough with the operation to be told more details without being bowled over. In this position, chances are better that you will get the full picture.
- Avoid the solution-only trap. You may have made it clear that you expect your employees to present problems only when they can offer a clear-cut course of action that you only need to approve or disapprove. Perhaps you did this to avoid the danger of their work being delegating upward to you. But there are times when your experience and grasp of wider possibilities can be valuable to this problem-solving process. So, be careful that your words and attitude do not indicate too quickly that you feel this is their problem, not yours. It is better to wait until you have discussed it before you decide.
- Reward the bearer. It is not easy to express enthusiasm when given a piece of bad news, but it is possible. The next time it happens, instead of wincing or saying: Why did not you tell me this sooner? You might try: I am glad you came to

---

Business Best Observation

A manager's chances of getting negative information from her employees depend on the kind of relationship she has developed and maintained. A hostile or remote attitude will prompt people to withhold information--even though it ultimately may be to the employees' disadvantage. But a friendly and sustained relationship encourages employees to come to the boss with whatever they think is important, good or bad.

me with this or this could have been much worse if you would waited before you told me. If you can make the bearer feel appreciated for doing the right thing, you can expect more of the same in the future.

HAS YOUR AUTHORITY SPRUNG A LEAK?

If you discover that your direct reports are taking their ideas or complaints straight to the higher-ups, you need to cultivate their trust and respect so they do not sabotage you. And while it may not offer much consolation, realize that you are not alone.

A recent survey by The Marlin Co., a North Haven, Conn., workplace communications firm, found that 33 percent of the respondents deem backstabbing a problem in their organization. Moreover, 30 percent believe that they have been a target of workplace gossip, and 24 percent have seen someone's reputation damaged by gossip or rumors. "Though many people consider gossip an amusing pastime, in reality it is disruptive and damaging," said Frank Kenna III, Marlin's president. "Most people engage in it, but they do not realize its consequences."

So if you overhear bits and pieces of conversations in which people who report to you are going behind your back, or you notice telling comments from your boss and cryptic glances from some employees, assess to what extent your team trusts you and has confidence in your leadership.

Although you are aware of what is happening, the real challenge is finding out why. You tell yourself that you are getting it from both sides, and that you have to find a way to put an end to it. What is the best approach to take in a situation like this?

NO HASTY MOVES

So far, you have realized an important truth for managers: the need to deal with an upsetting and potentially dangerous situation. Failure to do so could lead to the undermining of your position in the organization and the eventual erosion of your authority. But whatever your present situation, it is unwise to act hastily. You might say or do something damaging that you would regret later.

Rather, you should take time to answer, as objectively as possible, these two important questions:

1. What kind of relationship do you have with your boss?

    Many people make the mistake of thinking that any working relationship--be it with a boss, a colleague or a subordinate--continues on an even keel. If it was good yesterday, it also must be good today. But most of these relationships veer in different directions from time to time--from good to bad to better--depending on people and circumstances.

    It could be, therefore, that the relationship between you and your boss is not what you thought it was. Perhaps you have done something to anger her. Or, maybe there is a kind of power play involved; your boss may actually be encouraging the staff to come directly to her in an attempt to gain more power and possibly do you in. Thinking over the situation may reveal some problems that you hadn't realized existed.

2. What kind of relationship do you have with your reports?

    There has to be some reason people circumvent their immediate bosses. Sometimes, of course, it may be just a ploy to ingratiate themselves with top management. More often, though, it is due to the subordinates' belief that their bosses do not want to listen to their ideas or complaints and do not want to be concerned with their problems, which they are not empowered to solve.

    Are you open with the people who report to you, and do they think they can be honest with you? Are you willing to do something about their complaints and assist them with their problems? Do you encourage people to come to you with ideas and suggestions? In analyzing the situation again--as objectively as possible--you may find that you have been raising barriers between yourself and those who report to you. Not intentionally perhaps, but nonetheless they are there.

In line with your evaluation of the situation, you may want to take the following steps:

- Get on a better footing with your boss. This will call for some decisive action on your part—you cannot expect your boss to make the first move. Make it a point to consult him on special problems. Discuss some of your ideas. Ask for backing on a project you would like to undertake. Do all this in person and in an open, friendly manner.

Should you discuss with your boss the fact that certain employees have been going behind your back? Probably not at first. But as your relationship improves, you might bring it up and conclude with: I would appreciate it if, when something like that occurs again, you would simply refer that person back to me.

- Encourage people to come to you. This may take some doing at first, particularly if you have fallen into the habit of shutting people off or out. You might start by calling them into your office to talk over a problem and stopping by their offices to discuss ideas. Your aim should be to make them feel that your door is open and that you are receptive to their thinking. Equally important, you should be ready to act on that thinking when appropriate--be it in dealing with a complaint, pushing for a solution to a problem or putting good ideas to immediate use.

Business Best Observation

When people come to realize that you are indeed in charge and ready and willing to hear them out, they'll likely have no further reason for going above you to your boss. They'll see you as the boss.

YOUR NEGATIVE COMMENTS CAN BACKFIRE

One measure of your success as a motivator is the number of positive and negative comments you make in a typical workday. Tony Alessandra, author of *Charisma* (Warner Books, 2000), finds that the most effective leaders speak in positive terms and limit their negative remarks. He urges people to adopt pausitiveness, the ability to pause before dishing out negative opinions or observations.

Yet the urge to make negative comments about coworkers can be hard to resist, especially when you want to share what you heard about a colleague's embarrassing error or vent about an executive's haughty behavior. You may want to say it, you may trust the discretion of your listener and your opinion may be founded in fact. But it is still in your best interest to bite your tongue and think it over before uttering a word.

THE TOXIC BOSS

As startling as it may seem, there is always the possibility that team members are not the problem at all, but you are--the boss. A toxic boss, like terrible chemicals, can be harmful and destructive to the team environment and not even be aware that there is a problem. First and foremost, to be effective, your employees and team members need to and actually must admire you; that does not mean that they have to like you personally. However, you are toxic when you confuse, humiliate or otherwise upset workers, and they actually tend to model your behavior. The net results is a mess.

The signs of toxicity are not necessarily obvious to managers or even to their bosses. But a good business coach (or your workers themselves) can reflect the problems that you personally bring to the workplace. Motivating your team to top performance means that a candid review of your behavior, at times, may be absolutely necessary. Consider the following signs:

- Higher employee turnover or absenteeism (employees avoid going to work)
- Increasingly critical of your team members
- More worker complaints, formal and informal
- Arguments with team members and your boss
- Fewer employees who seek your advice
- Less measurable productivity and profitability
- Decreased personal satisfaction with your job
- Increased interpersonal conflict outside of the workplace

Difficult situations require immediate remedial action. And, of course, in this situation it is not other team members, but you, the boss, that needs remediation. If you begin to get insight that you are the problem, first and foremost, do not panic, but take a deep breath and calm down. Self-recrimination helps no one. Try to identify the symptoms: learn when and where your behavior and your management is out of place and how it produces negative results rather than positive outcomes.

In addition, you need to get objective feedback: consider discussing the situation with a trusted friend, your spouse, a business coach or even another manager within your organization. (A good deal of trust is required if your feedback comes from someone works at the same company as you do. Be sure that you have the right person and that this process will not become gossip at the water cooler.) Finally, the real task is to find what the critical behavior is: impatient, verbally abusive, worry, personal fear, lack of motivation or all of the above.

When you take action, do it with conviction. Work with your mentor, friend or coach to identify the problem--both must be in agreement of what is the cause before you can change. Understand why you want to change your behavior: It may be nothing more than you wish to keep your job! Decide what you can do about it and set up a realistic schedule to change your behavior. Bad habits are not cured in a week or even a month. As you begin to change your management style, reward yourself for your efforts. Everyone works better and more effectively if they get reinforcement; treat yourself well for your new you.

IN HARM'S WAY

For a variety of reasons, the negative sentiments you convey about others can do you direct harm. Consider some possibilities:

- You could have it wrong, particularly if what you are passing on is something you heard from someone else.
- Circumstances could change. The person could become your colleague--or even your boss--tomorrow.
- You could be incurring distrust. Speaking negatively about someone could by itself be what impresses your listeners the most, not necessarily the content of what you are saying. Listeners could well be forming negative impressions of you: for example, that you are indiscreet or might talk about them the same way.
- Your words could be used against you. Even if you are talking in confidence to

Business Best Observation

Saying only nice things is nice but not a good idea. Sometimes it is useful to convey negative information. But a particular tone of voice, a shrug or a conspicuous silence can convey a great deal about what you are thinking without getting yourself into trouble unnecessarily. If you must speak ill of someone, give the possible reaction some thought. It could prevent a lot of harm later.

someone you trust, you never know when or to whom your words will be repeated or misquoted.

- Your negativity could be equated with your attitude. Your remarks may be funny, apt and accurate, but as the saying goes, nobody likes a wise guy. People are put off by those who continually treat serious matters as a joke or who never pass up the chance to criticize a colleague or boss.

REHAB FOR A WHITE ELEPHANT

Tina, an elephant, lived in New York's Central Park Zoo for many years. When the zoo closed for remodeling, all the other large animals were easily placed in other zoos. But Tina exhibited such aggressive behavior against her keepers that no zoo wanted her until, finally, Marine World/Africa USA in Redwood City, Calif., took her. Tina thrived there. She learned to lie down on command, raise her feet and salute with her trunk. In fact, her hostility seemed to disappear, so the park even contemplated using her for children's rides.

It is not uncommon for managers to inherit a staff that includes a Tina, someone whose performance fails to meet their standards but who, for one reason or another, is difficult to move out. Like Tina, they stand in the way of whatever remodeling you have in mind. You have got to do something in a situation like this if you do not want to transfer or terminate a Tina. Below are some suggestions.

A new direction

Often people with talent and ability are not challenged enough to produce their best. They may have been slotted into a limited job by an unsympathetic or vindictive boss, maneuvered out of the mainstream by a rival or stigmatized by an unfairly acquired reputation.

As someone new to the scene, you are in a position to view such people in a fresh light, to take stock of their capabilities, accomplishments, ideas and interests.

One manager reports: I inherited some problem employees when I took over my present responsibilities. One of them--a traffic coordinator--had the reputation of being uncooperative and somewhat abrasive. However, in a conversation, I found her pleasant and interesting to talk to, although a bit defensive. I also found out she was enrolled in a computer course. I suspect this was because she felt her days with the company were numbered, and she wanted to be prepared to look for work elsewhere. Because I was already planning to computerize much more heavily than we had been, I asked her to do some research. The upshot is that she is now the operation's data processing supervisor and doing quite a job. I have not heard any more talk about the so-called negative aspects of her personality.

Encouragement

Blocked opportunities, repetitive work, low expectations--all these tend to produce boredom that verges on hopelessness, a belief that nothing significantly positive can happen on the job. Yet, no matter how deeply these feelings affect the employee, studies show that encouragement from above can produce a new direction.

One form of encouragement is to ask employees their opinions of what the operation might need to be more effective. Celeste Ford provides a good example. Ford runs Stellar Solutions, Inc., a $10 million aerospace-engineering services firm in Palo Alto, Calif. She is always asking for her workers' input on how to boost efficiency and improve results. Every year, Ford invites all her employees to a meeting where they help shape the company's strategic three-year plan. "It is like having all our employees on our board of directors," Ford says. "They are all helping set our direction."

To take another example, a line supervisor who is now deeply involved in his company's quality assurance program says, "Instead of simply giving me a production schedule and control sheet, the new general manager asked me how I thought the line could be improved. Then, after I had mentioned a couple of things, he suggested I put them into practice. It is helped a lot to get that kind of support."

A feeling of empowerment

Yours may be an operation in which employees have been too closely supervised and given little opportunity for independent action. This sort

Overcome Obstacles

Business Best Observation

Some managers assume that their operations are too limited to offer more scope to their employees, and that transfer or termination is the only solution to unsatisfactory performance. Yet, even when the budget is scant, they can try something new. It will be worth the effort.

of constraint can inhibit energy, ideas and the willingness to make a commitment. Often, even a small move away from oversupervision can produce surprising results.

An accountant who now supervises corporate accounts payable says that it was not until was not until he was put in charge of one customer's accounts payable that he realized how much he enjoyed being his own boss.

SHORT ON SENSITIVITY?

Empathy helps managers earn their employees' respect. By making a concerted effort to understand what people think and believe—and by seeing the situation from their point of view--you gain their trust. That sounds simple, but many managers fall short in terms of their ability to empathize.

In a study of 21 derailed executives, one personality flaw led all the rest. Insensitivity to others was the chief reason these managers failed to advance in their careers, according to Morgan W. McCall and Michael M. Lombardo, behavioral scientists at the Center for Creative Leadership in Greensboro, N.C.

Jacques A. Nasser, the former CEO of Ford Motor Co. who was forced out after the company's financial results plummeted during his watch, admitted in a *New York Times* interview that his people skills worked against him. "I should have been a little more sensitive about some of the stakeholders," he said.

AVOIDING THE SORE SPOTS

If you sometimes wonder why oversensitive people seem bent on taking your every word the wrong way, here is what you might be overlooking:

- Employees' egos are large--possibly larger than your own. If you ignore them when they need recognition, criticize them when they are hoping for praise or demean them when they want support, they are going to perceive your behavior as a threat to their self-esteem.

- Just as the forces of the body rush to combat an infection, so does the mind move to defend against a threat to the ego. If you do not foresee such defense building by others or fail to regard it as natural and legitimate, you might be in for some unpleasant surprises.
- People's sensitivities can be extensive, and it is not a bad idea to do as much mental cataloging of them as possible. If you do not know what they might be, ask for some advice from those who do.
- Relationships are not static. Sometimes they are only as good as your last conversation. It can be dangerous to assume that your rapport with another person is fine and that you no longer have to think about it. It is usually at this point when you find yourself stepping on toes, disregarding sensitivities and incurring resentment.

Your words can be upsetting unless you take pains to avoid angering those affected by them. For instance, if you are about to issue a critique of an employee's performance, it is better to indicate why it is coming: I would like to talk to you about something that needs some improvement. You may encounter disagreement, but you lessen the chances that the person will feel victimized.

Negative feelings can escalate, especially when you wait too long to show remorse for making a thoughtless remark. Your action does not necessarily have to be an apology, but at least it should open the door to a better understanding. You can ask if someone is angry with you, for instance. That way, your initial mistake would not turn into a feud, helped along perhaps by your feeling that you can be just as angry as he can.

Business Best Observation

Sensitivities are often trampled on by a manager who insists on a course of action without consulting those who will be most affected. Allowing others to change your mind is not a sign of weakness. Nor is consulting others. Rather, you enable them to have a voice. This kind of sharing is good management because it tends to dissolve resentment.

CURBING DISSENSION IN THE RANKS

In many companies, salespeople can qualify for lavish perks that are not available to other employees. Bruce Smith decided to fix that at his Houston-based video surveillance firm, Safety Vision.

Overcome Obstacles

Smith sensed rumblings of dissension as his customer service reps felt unappreciated and jealous of the kudos the sales force received. So now he gives each salesperson a blue poker chip to award to a service rep each month for exceptional effort. Recipients can cash in their chips by reaching into a hat and pulling out a prize, ranging from gift certificates to expensive pens.

Smith launched the program to foster teamwork and collaboration between the sales and service staff. The program has worked well in reducing internal bickering. Now everyone's pulling for one another's success.

Keep in mind that people who work together do not necessarily have to be on good terms. Indeed, some employees can work competently and productively with those they actually dislike. The way staff members feel about each other need not be a matter of great concern to a manager unless the animosity gets out of hand.

What is out of hand? Consider these situations:

- Key staffers are not speaking to each other.
- Hostile camps exist.
- Who does what has become a matter of who is friendly with whom.
- Staffers resist assignments outside their traditional ones.
- A small subgroup is closely holding key information.

DEFUSING A FEUD

If counterproductive situations exist in your group, you probably need to intervene. A thoughtful manager can reduce the effects of feuding and political positioning, but it is not easy.

Some suggestions to get you started:

- Make your message clear. You want people to cooperate. The staff will heed this message the most if the hostilities in your group are not widespread but limited to only two or three people. Consider holding a small, informal meeting to discuss the ongoing problem.
- Be equitable in your attention so that those who are feuding do not think you are taking sides. This action, along with your previous directive to cooperate, will strengthen your point.

- Tell them what you want. Sometimes a direct order is most effective. Sit down with feuding employees and discuss how animosity is hampering their work and upsetting others. Offer whatever assistance they feel is needed to iron out the issues between them.
- Identify a common cause. People who are at odds can be brought together by a common purpose. This could be some healthy competition with another organization or a deadline that is in everyone's interest to meet.
- Restructure jobs so that people must cooperate to accomplish their objectives. Or, if you decide that working together is impossible, find ways of making their work autonomous so they need not depend on each other to complete the assignment.

Business Best Observation

There also are situations in which you, the manager, can do nothing to help. In such cases, it is undoubtedly best that those involved work it out for themselves--provided the job is getting done.

MAKE GRIPE SESSIONS PAY OFF

Let us all get together on Tuesday morning for a no-holds-barred discussion. Problems, ideas, gripes--you name it, and we will talk about it. Many managers send out this kind of directive from time to time with the hope of gaining some valuable feedback. But frequently, those hopes do not materialize.

The staff may look at the session as a waste of time. It is just something the boss feels has to be done, they reason, and nothing will come of it anyway. So they keep their important ideas, their real gripes, to themselves. What is the point of making waves?

Getting the staff to speak freely

You may wonder, then, how you can turn people on at a session like this and convince them that you want to hear what is on their minds. Consider these suggestions:

- Keep the meeting small. The larger the meeting, the easier it is for people who are reluctant to speak up to fade into the crowd. They keep silent while others talk. Yet, they may be the ones who need to air their ideas and problems. It is not easy to hide, however, at a small meeting. So if you have a large staff reporting to you, hold two or three small sessions rather than an all-inclusive one. You will get a lot more straight talk, even if you have to prod.

- Hold the session in the round. A round table that can accommodate everyone is the ideal. If not, arrange the chairs in a circular fashion. The aim is to have close eye contact, which leads to maximum interaction. People are much more likely to respond when they can see one another. Furthermore, you fit into the group as a participant rather than as the boss.

- Listen intently. This is one situation you do not want to dominate. It is their talk session, not yours. Still, you do not want to come across as uninvolved. So when someone asks you a question or looks to you for a response, paraphrase what is been said as you start to reply. You will be demonstrating your attentiveness and encouraging more discussion.

- Put it in writing. From the outset of the meeting, take notes. This will indicate to the staff that you are indeed serious about hearing what they have to say. They also may view it as a hopeful sign that you are going to do something about particular issues mentioned. You can further strengthen this impression by asking for more specifics. If there is a complaint, for instance, ask for pertinent details; then say you will look into the matter and report back.

- Use a flip chart or blackboard. This technique can loosen the tongues of the most reluctant participants. If the discussion is slow in getting started or begins to bog down, go to the chart or board and lay the groundwork. Tell the team that you want to get some important points down, and that they can just throw out anything that is bothering them, anything at all. As you jot down their comments, keep your back to the group. People feel less threatened and freer to speak their minds when their boss is not facing them directly.

Business Best Observation

All the factors above are important in keeping an open session alive and kicking. But what about the next one? Will it be energized, too? The answer depends on what you do about their comments in the first meeting. So as it draws to a close, review your notes aloud to ensure you have everything straight. Then follow up and report back to those concerned. This is insurance for your credibility and for another meeting that will be just as productive as the first.

Appendix 1
Resources

HELP FOR SMALL BUSINESS OWNERS AND MANAGERS

For years, *Entrepreneur* magazine has been one of the mainstays for information, new ideas, trends and a wide variety of resources for entrepreneurs and small businesses. This hugely successful organization has expanded its reach in recent years, creating an enormous Website. While much of the material that can be found here is beyond the scope of this book, there are excellent (and free) articles and content on a variety of topics which can assist you in building the best possible workplace team you can. Do spend some time at this site, as a little effort in searching will be well worth your while. Visit www.entrepreneur.com for additional information.

By their own words, The National Federation of Independent Business is the leading advocacy organization representing small and independent businesses. A nonprofit, nonpartisan organization founded in 1943, NFIB represents the consensus views of its members in Washington and all 50 state capitals.

NFIB's mission is to promote and protect the right of its members to own, operate and grow their businesses. NFIB also gives its members a power in the marketplace. By pooling the purchasing power of its members, the National Federation of Independent Business gives members access to many business products and services at discounted costs. NFIB also provides timely information designed to help small businesses succeed. Their Website is a rich resource for all aspects of small business management, including the themes of motivation and retention. For more information on this great site, visit *www.nfib.com*. Click the tab in the upper right called Tools & Tips for access to their articles and management suggestions.

There are some popular and useful sites that, while devoted to all aspects of small business, are nevertheless helpful in matters of motivating and influencing employee behavior through constructive and proactive management. Consider visiting any of the following sites:

A Better Workplace, *www.abetterworkplace.com*

All Business, *www.allbusiness.com*

Business Owner's Toolkit, *www.toolkit.cch.com*

Employer-Employee, *www.employer-employee.com*

Inc, *www.inc.com*

SCORE, *www.score.org*

Small Business Administration, *www.sba.gov*

Small Business info Canada, *www.sbinfocanada.about.com*

Small business owners and managers who want to motivate and manage for top performance may find some of the following books useful and informative:

50 plus one Tips When Hiring and Firing Employees, Encouragement Press, 2006

Create Your Own Employee Handbook: A Legal & Practical Guide, Nolo, 2005

Increasing Productivity and Profit in the Workplace, Wiley, 2001

Motivation and Goal Setting: How to Set and Achieve Goals and Inspire Others, Career Press, 1998

Stop Hiring Failures, BookSurge Publishing, 2006

HIRING, DEVELOPING AND TRAINING TEAM MEMBERS

For the hiring process to work effectively, it must be accomplished with sensitivity and care, but also legally. A number of sites on the Internet sell basic forms and documents for hiring, training, firing and legal compliance. In particular, there are templates for employee manuals which are easy to use and can be readily adapted to your company needs--and they are inexpensive. Visit *www.socrates.com* for a ready-to-use employment manual and all the other employments needed to manage the hiring process correctly from the start.

Starting employees off well from the beginning is one of the most important steps a manager can take to ensure top team performance. On-boarding, the process of integrating new team members, is a particularly effective and useful approach. Visit *www.humancapitalinstitute.org* for a free Webcast series about on-boarding. There are also a number of other organizations that offer tools for automating the on-boarding process; simply search the Internet using the phrase, on-boarding.

There are a large number of useful and informative books on the subjects of hiring, developing and training team members. Here are a few that readers have found helpful in building their management skills, vis-à-vis improving team morale and employee performance:

Employee Fringe and Welfare Benefit Plans, Thomson-West, 2005

How to Start a Training Program, ASTD, 1999

Instant Team Building, Instant Success, McGraw-Hill, 2005

Organizing a Conference, Jalco Publishing House, 2005

Retreats that Work: Everything You Need to Know about Planning and Leading Great Offsites, Pfeiffer, 2006

Turning Training Into Learning: How to Design and Deliver Programs that Get Best Results, AMACOM, 2000

Writing Training Materials that Work: How to Train Anyone to Do Anything, Pfeiffer, 2003

HELP WITH DIFFICULT MANAGEMENT SITUATIONS

Every manager or owner, at one time or another, needs help to solve what can be affectionately referred to as sticky situations--conflict, hostility, dissent, poor communication, poor attitude...well, you get the point. In and of themselves, none of these items will bring down the ship; but they sure can rock the place much more often than anyone wants.

There are a number of very productive and useful Websites which can assist. All of these will be useful in motivating your team to top performance, which is the ultimate goal of this book and all the suggestions it contains.

ABetterWorkplace.Com is in its 21st year of helping make workplaces work better through practical tools, new strategies and inspiration for approaching challenging professional situations. This site offers resources and ideas to guide innovative and lasting solutions to sticky workplace, business and people problems. Among the many functional and useful features of this site are that after registering, you can view an extensive selection of articles and handy tips; review course offerings and outlines for your personal and professional improvement (and for your workers, of course); receive a free electronic newsletter and see a list of new, hot books which may be useful for operating managers. For more information, visit *www.abetterworkplace.com*.

Performance appraisals, particularly with problem or under-performing employees, can be tricky business for any manager, no matter how skilled or experienced. But there is help and there are several Websites available to guide you in developing your own performance appraisal system. Consider the following sites: *www.bronline.com*, *http://performance-appraisals.org* and *www.blr.com*. If internal development is not reasonable, companies such as Hewitt,

PeopleSoft and Parthenon Group specialize in human resource problems and solutions. If you choose to outsource your performance management system needs, these companies can tailor a specific system to your company's needs.

Progressive discipline is a standard and fairly benign approach to working with under-performing employees in a way that benefits both the company and the employee. Several Websites that extensively cover human resource issues also have sections devoted to this specific topic. Visit the following sites for more information: *www.humanresources.about.com*, *www.allbusiness.com* and *www.citebr.com*.

Readers may find the following books useful in working through difficult management situations:

How to Manage Problem Employees: A Step-by-Step Guide for Turning Difficult Employees into High Performers, Wiley, 2005

Why Employees Don't Do What They're Suppose to Do and What You Can Do About It, McGraw-Hill, 1999

Discipline without Punishment: The Proven Strategy that Turns Problem Employees into Superior Performers, AMACOM, 2006

Resources